THE PSYCHOANALYSIS OF DREAMS

ÁNGEL GARMA

THE PSYCHOANALYSIS *OF* DREAMS

WITH AN INTRODUCTION BY

BERTRAM D. LEWIN

Jason Aronson New York

First Aronson Edition

Translated from the Spanish by the author.
Originally published as *Psicoanálisis de los Sueños,*

Reprinted by arrangement with Quadrangle Books, Inc.
Library of Congress Catalog Card Number: 73-17741
ISBN: 0-87668-118-6

Printed in U.S.A. by
NOBLE OFFSET PRINTERS, INC.
New York, N.Y. 10003

Acknowledgment

First, I thank my patients, who in their psychoanalytic sessions told me the dreams included in this book and the thoughts associated with those dreams which made my interpretations possible.

I also thank my friends and colleagues who discussed with me my work on dreams, particularly the theory about traumatic situations in the genesis of dreams and other hallucinations.

Among these many friends I would like to mention Dr. Alfred Flarsheim of Chicago, who encouraged this American edition, gave me many helpful suggestions and criticisms, and made many valuable corrections of the English translation.

Mrs. Shulamith Calles deserves my deep gratitude for her constant and clever endeavors to improve the translation and for keeping the manuscript and printer's proofs free of stylistic and typographical mistakes.

Grateful acknowledgment is made to the editors of the *International Journal of Psychoanalysis* for permission to reprint my articles: "The Traumatic Situation in the Genesis of Dreams" (Chapter 6) and "Dreams in Color" (end of Chapter 5), as well as to the editor of the *Psychoanalytic Quarterly* for the articles: "The Genesis of Dream Hallucination" (Chapter 7) and "The Dream Screen and the Isakower Phenomenon" (Chapter 8). Also to the editor of the *Revista de Psicoanalisis* of Buenos Aires where some other parts of the book were first published.

I also feel very much indebted to my wife for her helpful encouragement and for her clearsighted psychoanalytic knowledge and judgment.

ÁNGEL GARMA

Buenos Aires

Preface

The intention of this book is to offer a gradual but at the same time profound approach to the practice and theory of the psychoanalytical interpretation of dreams.

It has its origins in my clinical psychoanalytical experience over a period of more than forty-five years, as well as in my teaching as professor of Psychoanalysis of Dreams at the Institute of Psychoanalysis in Buenos Aires. The dreams I describe are from my analysands who also helped me with their free associations in the task of interpretation. I have repeatedly discussed the contents of this book with the doctors who are students at the Institute. Under these circumstances points which prove difficult to grasp become evident, enabling me to expound them in an ever more accessible form.

My teaching vocation has led me to include in this book some drawings of dreams, which are in addition quite easy to produce, since dreams are above all visual phenomena of highly concrete content. There is also another reason. Occasionally, and perhaps to some slight degree in all cases, when dealing with dream material, one is likely to suffer a certain drowsiness. This is clearly shown in the drawing in the chapter dealing with the dream screen. This is due to the fact that dreams originate in repressed contents which arouse resistance. It is also basically caused because dreams originate in the sleeping state and therefore somehow tend to be conducive to that state. My experience with courses and lectures has offered repeated proof that the exposition of dreams with the help of drawings made by actual dreamers helps to keep my listeners alert and enables them to obtain an empathetic understanding of the interpretations.

The other graphic material consists of artistic expressions of different levels. Some of the works of art are world famous, others of a commercial nature, and still others are typical of somewhat more popular art forms. All this graphic material displays in a clearly discernible form the same primitive psychological elaborations which in dreams appear very enigmatic. This difference is due to the fact that in the graphic material these elaborations appear in order to be understood, whereas in dreams their function is to conceal repressed genetic content. By comparing this other graphic material with the drawing of dreams, these elaborations can be demonstrated in a very objective manner, and the study of their symbolism, whose interpretation in dreams often meets with skepticism and rejection, is also made possible.

In the interpretation of the dreams drawn in this book something extremely important in psychoanalytical treatment becomes clearly apparent, namely, the transferential relationship between the analysand and his analyst.

The book opens with a study of the dreams that are drawn and the other graphic material. Supported by this, I go on to present the general psychoanalytical theory of dreams.

The most original theoretical contributions of this book center on the two chapters that deal with the traumatic situations that give rise to dreams and the genesis of dream hallucination. In the first case, on the basis of Freud's teachings, I challenge Freud's own definition of dreams as the fulfillment of repressed wishes. In preference, I defend my hypothesis that dreams are disguised unconcious traumatic situations which can neither be tolerated in their true form nor totally repressed due to the sleeping state of the individual. In the other chapter I analyze the phenomenon of hallucination, which is to say the belief that what one is dreaming is reality, an essential characteristic of dreams. I believe I can offer an explanation of the origin of this phenomenon by means of a reversal of Freud's hypothesis concerning reality testing, this being the psychological function that enables us to distinguish a perception arising from stimuli of the external reality from the perception of a fantasy. The origin of hallucinations occurring in other mental disturbances, such as traumatic neuroses, is also thereby clarified.

Two of the book's chapters are in the nature of psychoanalytical research. In one I consider the dream screen discovered by B. D. Lewin. I begin the other by referring to dreams of a type which are recurrent in clinical practice, namely, those which symbolize pregnancy and childbirth with articles of clothing or pieces of cloth. Directing my attention to these garments and materials I was able to discover that they symbolize fetal membranes. This discovery surprised me since it was totally unexpected. On the basis of my findings in this type of dream and also in folklore referring to pregnancy and childbirth I came to the conclusion that the idea of clothing originates in the desire of prehistoric mothers to find a substitute for their fetal membranes so that their newborn children might continue to enjoy the same protection that they were given in the womb. In the same way tattooing and virtually all body ornamentation has a maternal origin; however, this situation changes when the individual reaches puberty and tends to identify with the father.

This book also describes the technique of interpretating dreams in the course of psychoanalytical treatment. In the final chapter I again deal with the importance of unconscious traumatic situations in the origin of dreams. The fact that one cannot control these situations when asleep brings every individual to believe in the reality of his dreams.

This book has not only been translated into English but also into French, which, together with the five Spanish editions have favored its diffusion and the scientific discussion of its contents. I fervently hope that this new American edition fulfills its didactic function and at the same time provides knowledge and understanding of my original ideas on dreams.

Ángel Garma

Buenos Aires, 1974

Contents

	Preface	vii
	Introduction by Bertram D. Lewin	xiii
1.	*Dreams and Their Psychoanalytic Interpretation*	21
2.	*The Dream Work*	42
3.	*Dreams in Psychoanalytic Treatment*	65
4.	*Genital Symbolism in Dreams*	71
5.	*Genital Conflicts*	104
6.	*The Traumatic Situation in the Genesis of Dreams*	128
7.	*The Genesis of Dream Hallucination*	141
8.	*The Dream Screen and the Isakower Phenomenon*	157
9.	*Deviations from Psychoanalytic Interpretation*	174
10.	*Reversing Freud's Theory*	194
	Bibliography	209
	Indexes to Dreams:	213
	A. Symbols	213
	B. Things Symbolized	218
	Index to the Book	221

Introduction

This book is not only a treatise on the psychoanalysis of dreams, as its title proclaims. It is also an event and a documentation; for Dr. Ángel Garma, who outlines the events of his career in his preface, has been not only an author but a historical figure in psychoanalysis. Events led him from his native Spain into many countries—to Germany for his psychoanalytic education, to France then as quasi-exile, finally in 1939 to Buenos Aires where he established himself. Later he was able to enjoy fruitful visits to England and to the United States, and in the latter country in Topeka, Kansas, he served for a term as Sloan Visiting Professor at the Menninger School of Psychiatry.

Thus Dr. Garma has had many "influences" play upon him and he too has been an important "influence." He has been among other things a cultured messenger.

Spanish and Portuguese America now have a vigorous and creative psychoanalytic movement. In Mexico and South America there are organized national psychoanalytic societies, institutes for psychoanalytic education, and an association of Latin American societies, and all of these are participants and contributors in the large world of psychoanalysis represented by the International Psychoanalytic Association. Psychoanalytic journals and psychoanalytic books are written and published by Latin Americans. The *Revista de Psicoanalisis* of Buenos Aires is now in its twenty-first year of publication.

In 1939, when Dr. Garma went to Buenos Aires from Europe, he could have seen little to suggest such efflorescence. There was no psychoanalyst in the city or indeed in the whole of Argentina. Europe and to a lesser extent the United States were still the psychoanalytic centers where a Latin American national might at times participate or exchange views with colleagues.

Dr. Garma became an influence then. He was a founder of the Argentine Psychoanalytic Society and of the *Revista.* He also in time became the founder of the Psychoanalytic Institute in Buenos Aires, its first director, and consistently since then a teacher. Besides such local activity, he has taken part in the world movement, attending congresses, writing (and having translated into other languages) various articles and books. His first psychoanalytic second country was Germany, since he received his training at the Berlin Psychoanalytic Institute, but France too came to figure later on, and in more recent years England and the United States, as the generous tribute in his preface shows, where he expresses appreciation of his North American friends and his pleasure in the American publication of *The Psychoanalysis of Dreams.*

This book too has a history. It was originally a pioneering job, its first Spanish edition *Psicoanálisis de los sueños* appearing in Buenos Aires in 1940, and it was reprinted and partly rewritten in 1948, 1956, and 1963. The various editions and versions no doubt represent the increasing sophistication of Dr. Garma's readers, and the present edition gives evidence of the different epochs. Thus the first five chapters, more nearly adhering to the original exposition, are elementary instruction and description. They come from Garma's early teaching years and were intended for a wide range of readers. These chapters give the rules of dream interpretation and expound the role of genitality in the construction of dream pictures. The dream manifest is usually a picture, and Garma hit upon the original didactic device of using drawings and paintings of dreams made by the dreamer. This was long before psychoanalytic teachers, at any rate, had been made aware of the value of pedagogy of "visual aids." Incidental to the clinical exposition, Garma also draws upon *belles lettres* and the visual arts for a large number of relevant and instructive illustrations.

The teacher's need to expound and organize often leads not only to novel methods of presentation but to a corollary awareness of new connections between the ideas he is expounding. Thus naturally, Garma too (in the subsequent chapters) came to see a new way of relating the old psychoanalytic and medical idea of trauma to the principles of dream formation. As he says, his views on the traumatic origin of dreams remain controversial, although Robert Fliess has pointed out that they are possibly new statements of Freud's position. I shall not attempt here a critique of this matter, nor of the contents of the remaining chapters. In them Garma brings his readers abreast of the new ideas about the dream, his own ideas as well as those of others. To my taste, the chapter on the dream screen and the Isakower phenomenon, where Garma again uses pictures to demonstrate the novel points in theory, is the most rewarding.

Thus this book contains expositions of the psychoanalytic interpretation of dreams that are derived from many sources. Both advanced and beginning readers will find food for thought and pleasant reading.

BERTRAM D. LEWIN

Pipersville, Pennsylvania, 1966

THE PSYCHOANALYSIS OF DREAMS

Chapter I

DREAMS AND THEIR PSYCHOANALYTIC INTERPRETATION

Dreams are hallucinations which occur during sleep. They are usually incomprehensible and soon forgotten. Freud has demonstrated that unfulfilled wishes are at the bottom of all dreams. For instance, we may find a hungry man dreaming of banquets and a thirsty man of overflowing rivers. The man in love dreams about his beloved, as we can see in an old Spanish poem:

Un sueño soñaba anoche,	I dreamed a dream last night,
Soñito del alma mía,	Dream of my heart,
Soñaba con mis amores	I dreamed of my love,
Que en mis brazos los tenía.	And held her in my arms.

But the psychology of dreams is more complicated than this simple verse. If it were only a question of wish fulfillment, as in the above dream, they would be perfectly understandable. But we have repeatedly found that this is not so.

The psychology of dreams is indeed more complicated because of the kinds of wishes manifested in them. Wishes which give rise to dreams are wishes which are repressed by the ego during the waking state because they are threatening to the individual. These wishes are often of an instinctual nature, with oral, anal, or genital aims; they derive from infantile levels of emotional development and do not seem to be normal to the dreamer himself.

The instinctual life of human beings is very complicated. All of us have a great many wishes which are repressed because they are involved in intrapsychic conflict. Perverse desires exist, in most cases unconsciously, which may be sadistic, masochistic, homosexual, or exhibitionistic.

All these desires aim at gratification, and if internal conflict prevents it, we know that some of the ego's energy has fought them and rejected them. It has been said that the difference between a criminal and an honest man is that the latter dreams of what the former actually does. Exaggerated as this view may be, it nevertheless carries some truth.

During the day these wishes are repressed by the efforts of the ego. But what happens at night? During sleep the ego relaxes its repressive control; consequently the repressed wishes, which do not sleep and retain their full force, reach consciousness more easily and may lead to a dream in which they are satisfied in a hallucinatory way.

For example, consider the extreme case of a person with intense repressed sadism who dreams during the night that he commits an act of cruelty. What would then happen? He would awake in anguish because not even in a dream could he bear to have that kind of wish satisfied.

We find then a conflict situation: on the one hand, in order to sleep the ego must fully rest and relax. This means that the ego must partially withdraw its energy from the functions it exercises during the day. But if the ego withdraws the energy with which it represses certain desires, they can then be satisfied in hallucinations. They can produce dreams which may cause anxiety and awaken the ego. Thus the following dilemma exists: if the ego does not withdraw its energy, it cannot sleep because it is in a state of tension; but it also cannot sleep if it withdraws its energy, because then anxiety dreams appear. This leads to the advice that Antonio Machado gives in a poem:

Malos sueños he,	Bad dreams have I,
Me despertaré.	'Tis best to awake.

But the ego needs to sleep and so must solve this dilemma. It does so by making the wish, which is satisfied in the dream, appear in a disguised form.

In concrete terms, this means that the man with repressed sadism would dream, for instance, about a killing, but in the dream he would appear as a mere spectator and not as the criminal. The crime would be committed in the dream by someone unknown to him. In other words, in the dream his own wishes would be projected and imputed to someone else. This projection would free him from anxiety and permit him to go on sleeping peacefully.

We can now formulate two essential characteristics of dream psychology: first, there are *repressed wishes* in dreams; and secondly, in dreams repressed wishes do not appear as they are, but first go through a process of *disguise* so that the ego will not recognize them and will be able to go on sleeping.

The following dream which an Austrian lady had during the war (a dream described by von Hug-Hellmuth) further illustrates the way in which wishes are disguised in dreams. It is not difficult to guess the repressed wish that gave rise to the dream, even though it is not clearly expressed. The lady dreamed that she went to a military hospital and told the sergeant on guard that she wished to speak to the doctor in charge, as she wished to undertake some duties in the hospital. She said the word "duty" in such a way that the sergeant realized she meant "love duties." The sergeant was rather reluctant to admit her, as she was an elderly lady and therefore not fit for "love duties." She went in, but instead of going to the doctor in charge, she reached a room full of officers and army doctors. She explained her wish to the captain, who quickly understood her. She expressed herself in the following way: "I and many other women and girls are ready to . . . (*here the dreamer heard nothing but murmuring in her dream*) with officers and soldiers, without regard to rank or class." Despite the murmuring, the men in the room fully understood what she meant, and she knew it by the faces they made. She continued, "I know our resolution puzzles you, but we have thought about it earnestly. The soldier on the battlefront is not asked either whether or not he wants to die." After this there was a painful silence. The captain put his arm round her waist and said, "Imagine. Madam, what will really happen, that you . . ." (*murmuring in the dream*). She removed the officer's arm, thinking that all men were the same, and added, "Good gracious! I am already an old woman and possibly with me nothing will happen . . ."

The dream is clear; its source is a sexual wish. If this older woman were to become aware of harboring such wishes, she would feel indignant. Therefore the wish is masked in the dream, if not for the listeners, at least for herself. The disguise is achieved by the substitution of murmuring for the actual expression of the wish which prompted the dream.

The question will invariably be raised as to why psychoanalysts always find a sexual meaning in dreams, although man also has other wishes. The answer is that psychoanalysts do not purposely seek sexual meanings in dreams, but experience has shown dreams to have them. This is not strange, for one might say that in adults most repressed wishes are of a sexual nature. Other kinds of wishes—for instance, the wish for food—are well accepted both by the ego and by society. But our society tolerates only certain kinds of sexual satisfaction, forcing all others to be repressed. So it is not strange that these wishes appear in dreams.

Another form of masking wishes in dreams is *symbolic representation:* an object or an act does not appear as it is but is represented by means of symbols. Although these symbols are numerous in dreams as well as in everyday life, it will suffice to mention just a few. Among the symbols of everyday life there are, for instance, the flag symbolizing a nation, the sword symbolizing the army, and scales symbolizing justice.

Dreams are full of symbols which may stand for close relatives, the human body (particularly the sexual organs and activities), and death. To quote a few examples: a parent may be symbolized in dreams by a king or queen, an emperor, a professor, or, in general, by a person of authority. The genital organs may be represented by objects which resemble them: elongated objects such as a sword, a lance, a torch, or a lantern may symbolize the male organ; objects which contain something, such as a wardrobe, a stove, or a room, may symbolize the female organ. A flower is also a frequent symbol for the female organ, as in the common expression "the flower of chastity." Genital activity is often symbolized by other activities, such as eating. That eating should be a symbol of intercourse is not strange to English-speaking people, for if a man admires a girl he is apt to say that she is "sweet" and that he could "eat her up"; but for a German such a symbolization must seem strange, just as other symbolizations which appear in dreams of other languages seem strange to us.

In short, repressed desires are the motives of dreams and are frequently masked by symbolic representations and other devices, such as *dramatization.*

In dreams there are no abstract thoughts but only concrete images—substitutions which are made without regard for conscious logical coherence. The abstract thoughts of a person who, in his mind, reviewed something that had happened to him, appeared in his dreams as pictures in a magazine. Another person dreamed of an event which had happened years ago, and the people were dressed in old-fashioned clothes. In another dream, a person's thought of becoming fifteen again took the form of giving back fifteen cents. A person expressed the thought of starting a new business by appearing in new clothes in his dream. Another person who thought people were putting obstacles in the way of his business dreamed of torpedoes next to his store, which meant that his business was being "torpedoed."

Perhaps to many people this explanation of certain dream processes will seem farfetched and artificial. This is precisely the impression that dreams produce when they are scrutinized by our conscious mind. But the psychoanalytic study of dreams proves beyond doubt that these mechanisms exist, not only in the formation of dreams but also in other psychological phenomena.

Choosing at random, for instance, some medical advertisements, one can clearly see how they use dramatization in precisely the same way as in dreams. A laxative is represented by the broken bar of a cell through which the prisoner has escaped (the cell symbolizes the rectum) [FIGURE 2]. Another advertisement expresses the same idea by showing a municipal street cleaning device [FIGURE 3]. The action of a blood circulation regulator is expressed pictorially by an apparatus which obliges two people to circulate in determined directions; one is dressed in blue and is plethoric, like the blood in the veins, and the other is thin and dressed in a red doctor's jacket, the color of arterial blood—and he smiles, giving us to understand that the doctor who uses the advertised drug will be able to cure circulatory disorders very satisfactorily [FIGURE 4]. The loss of vitality in the menopause is represented by a woman missing a train, the last coach of which has broken loose [FIGURE 5]. We can now see that dreaming of missing a train means, as it does in the advertisement, missing some opportunity in life, generally an opportunity of an amorous nature.

Dramatization can, of course, also be seen in many other advertisements. For instance, the fact that a certain make of electric bulb uses little electricity is shown by the concrete image of a canoe going downstream taking advantage of the current [FIGURE 6].

Symbols appear not only in dreams but also in advertisements, literature, folklore, jokes and other communications. Flowers, frequently symbolizing the female genitals, have the same meaning in advertisements: on a poster for a product which regulates the menstrual cycle, flowers are placed at equal distances, indicating regularity; a red petal symbolizes menstruation [FIGURE 7]. Another similarity between these advertisements and dreams is that the woman is shown to one side, independent of the symbol for her genital organ.

Sometimes the symbolized meaning is too obvious [FIGURE 8]; at other times, a small detail in a situation is seized upon and inordinately dramatized. This is the case in an advertisement for a cold remedy, which shows three handkerchiefs drying on a line [FIGURE 9]. This exaggeration of a small detail occurs frequently in dreams.

In order to discover the meaning of a dream, the dreamer himself must be encouraged to impart his ideas, but as he himself is not consciously aware of the meaning, an indirect technique must be used. The dream may be divided into its different components and the dreamer may be asked to communicate his thoughts relating to each fragment. Thus, associations emerge which slowly intermingle and gradually permit insight into the wishes behind the dream. During psychoanalytic treatments, when a dream is reported during a session, it is usual to relate it with what the patient reports both before and after it. The analyst tries to find the latent connections between all the material of the session. If by this means he is unable to understand the dream, he has recourse to the patient's associations with the partial components of the dream, many of which have a multiple significance.

But another fact should be kept in mind in order to understand dreams occurring in the course of psychoanalytic treatment. During treatment the patient develops strong feelings and ideas relating to the analyst; for instance, the patient hates or "falls deeply in love" with the doctor. This reaction is known as *transference.* Whenever the patient manifests these feelings, the therapist's work must focus on investigating the motives which led the patient to react in this fashion; that is, he must *analyze the transference.* In other words, in analysis the positive and negative transference reactions are discussed with the patient, just as his other psychological symptoms are discussed. We then usually find that feelings connected with the transference originate in the patient's childhood and were subsequently directed toward persons whom the analyst now represents for various reasons. (We shall return later to a discussion of positive transferences.)

In order to interpret dreams, the psychoanalyst must rely on the patient's associations to the dream; he must try to find connections between the dream and whatever the patient discloses during sessions, since thoughts which come at random, without apparent relation to the dream, frequently provide the key to its understanding. On communicating his associations, the dreamer must overcome a resistance established by repressing forces which reject the work of interpretation. To encourage the dreamer to pursue the study of his dreams and overcome the initial resistance which always exists, it is sometimes helpful to suggest that he draw them or write them down. But this should be done only after associations to the dream have been obtained during the psychoanalytic session. Although the drawing of dreams is generally of little interpretive value, it is of some didactic value in clarifying the psychoanalytic method of dream interpretation, because drawings fix the dream image in the mind better than a simple description. For this reason I reproduce here a patient's drawings of her dreams and their description, together with the associations and the interpretation found in subsequent psychoanalytic sessions.

The patient was a young woman whose psychological history cannot be given for reasons of professional discretion. She had intense marital conflicts which she was unable to resolve satisfactorily and which finally led to divorce. In the following dream her difficult marital situation is described but transferred to the psychoanalytical situation: *

1] *I see a narrow oval hall.* [FIGURE 10]. *There is a second floor with a railing of the same shape as the hall. The thin bars are painted black. There is a lot of light. I am dressed. Several people are seated next to the railing, I among them. I am waiting for something. Suddenly a man comes out through a door in front of me. He is naked. He is a strange shape; his color is greenish yellow. I look at him, frightened. He approaches the group. He comes near me. With a pair of bellows, violently and quickly, he blows white powder over my back and then goes away.*

* We have not followed a strictly chronological order in these dreams, in order to facilitate the study of different interpretations.

It is an interesting dream and, through its symbolism, easy to understand. "To put powder" is a common Argentine expression indicating intercourse. The bellows are a phallic symbol and the narrow oval hall represents the female sex. The thin black bars which form a railing stand for the pubic hair. A "lot of light" means that much is expected from marriage and also from psychoanalysis; but the greenish yellow color suggests something sickly to the dreamer, and the man in the dream is her own husband. Thus one can deduce that the dream reproduces intercourse with the husband, whom she regards as sick—a traumatic situation which caused anxiety.

In this dream, as in many others, the coitus is *a tergo*. The group of women represents the dreamer herself; there are several women because the traumatic situation with the husband occurred repeatedly. (The husband also represents the psychoanalyst, whom she has also seen several times, but not for as long as she would have liked.) Dreams often utilize this technique of reproducing a given situation with some circumstance repeated several times to indicate that this particular circumstance had occurred on more than one occasion. The interpretation of this technique tends at first to be disconcerting because the conscious mind hardly considers it a logical way of expression. But we should remember that the rules of logic governing the conscious mind disappear in the unconscious, which is the seat of dreams.

The manifest content of the dream is also disconcerting, because the female genital organ is symbolized by a room and the dreamer by someone inside it—the very opposite of the real situation in which the genital organ is inside the person. The same thing happens in many dreams, for instance, when in the manifest content a person finds himself on the flat roof of his house; in terms of the symbolism, roof equals head, and it may mean that he is taken up with his own thoughts. From such psychological observations one must deduce that many dreams represent the genital organ with the dreamer in it in order to express the ego's actual concentration upon it. This is rather analogous to a situation in which a person is so completely preoccupied with an intricate problem when awake, that he feels his whole personality is concentrated in his head, while the rest of his body does not exist.

The dream we have described reproduces the traumatic situation of unsatisfactory intercourse with the husband, which constitutes one of the reasons for the patient's present neurosis. This finding confirms what psychoanalysis has so often shown to be true: that a neurosis is always a consequence of the failure to find the libidinous satisfaction so necessary for a normal life.

Psychoanalysis has further shown that two kinds of failure must exist in order for a neurosis to develop: one external, the other of intrapsychic origin. This was the case with the young woman whose dreams we are studying. Apart from the external marital failure there was also an internal failure: she was incapable of finding normal instinctual gratification in coitus because of unresolved infantile conflicts.

Living under normal conditions, our patient might have been able to overcome these inner inhibitions, but the failure of her marriage merely reactivated and strengthened them. On the other hand, if these inhibitions had not existed, or rather if she had not been incapable of solving her internal libidinous conflicts, she might have been able to overcome her marital difficulties, or at least lead a different kind of life.

It is this inner failure which gave rise to the following anxiety dream [FIGURES 11 AND 12]:

2] *I go on board. I am on board. The ship begins to toss, and the stern bangs first to the left against the wharf, then to the right against some cases. The ship moves so much I cannot keep my feet. I get seasick. Some people notice it and advise me to go to bed. I think they are right and take the elevator to the fourth floor to lie down, but before I can get there, the ceiling of the elevator and the floor move toward each other and I feel I shall be squashed. I want to save myself and, despairing of doing so, I awake.*

The first part of the patient's dream represents her anxiety about intercourse: she herself, through associations, interpreted the cases as the male sexual glands, since the Spanish word for "cases" (*cajones*) resembles a vulgar word for the male sexual glands (*cojones*). Vulgar expressions of this kind appear in dreams because the repression of such words is overcome during sleep.*

The ship in which the dreamer is sailing symbolizes her own genital organs, and to "go on board" means deciding to have intercourse. This decision appears in the dream as a dramatization of the common expression "to embark upon an undertaking."

The fact that she is represented inside the boat means, as in the previous dream, that at that moment she is preoccupied with genital excitation. The dream portrays a situation which arouses anguish and anxiety, and it expresses this by means of dramatization, as in the common expression "to be up against the wall." It also signifies the patient's finding herself between the male genital organ and the bed during intercourse.

Continuing the examination of the manifest content of the dream, we find that the people who perceive her anxiety advise her to go and rest. These people represent friends of the patient.

---

* It is easy to present more examples of this kind of dream. In the following dream, which is of a sexually unsatisfied married woman, the same vulgar word as in the previously quoted dream is again repressed, with the same dream elaboration to avoid censorship.

3] *I open the drawer of my husband's desk and find a billfold with pink banknotes in it. I ask my husband why he keeps that money there.*

It is a dream caused by unsatisfied genital wishes. The drawer (in Spanish, *cajon*) is similar to a vulgar word, *cojon,* which means the male sexual glands, and the bills represent the valuable contents of these. Apart from representing love, the pink of the bills symbolizes flesh and blood, which in this case are represented by the seminal excretion.

Analogous elaborations are produced by obscene words of anal origin.

From the subsequent course of the dream and the patient's drawing of it, it was deduced that "to go and rest" meant to have psychoanalytic treatment and free herself of her anxiety. In the manifest content of the dream this idea is represented by the words "to rest," because the patient lies on a couch, as if resting, during her psychoanalytic sessions. This interpretation is confirmed by the fact that the fourth floor, alluded to in the manifest content of the dream with no relation to anything previously expressed, is the floor on which her doctor lives; moreover, the drawing of the elevator, which has a special shape, can easily be recognized as the elevator in the analyst's house.

Thus, in the dream, the patient undergoes psychoanalytic treatment, and the events of the dream correspond to reality, inasmuch as treatment was not able to relieve her anxiety rapidly. On the contrary, at first the treatment brought on new conflicts which came from the need to express all her thoughts —even those which she found unpleasant—and from her affective transference. All this made her sad and *depressed*. These feelings were represented in the dream by the lowering of the ceiling of the elevator, which *pressed down* on her and threatened to squash her.

This anxiety dream upset the patient greatly because in it she could see no solution to her conflicts. Even the drawing of it elicited her anxiety. To overcome her anxiety, even if only by magical means, she felt obliged to make another drawing of the same dream giving it a brighter, rosier, and more pleasant appearance. Moreover, in the new drawing the cases are not piled up quite as high, and an exit from the previously closed-in cabin is now visible. This modification in the dream content was made several days later and illustrates what is termed the "secondary revision" of a dream. In other cases this secondary revision is less apparent and often unnoticeable.

The men in the new drawing of the dream are more erect. Psychoanalytic interpretation had shown that the drooping heads and hanging arms of the first drawing referred to impotence; the arm and head symbolized the penis. In the second drawing the impotence is corrected.

Briefly, these two dreams indicate that external and intrapsychic failures resulting in a neurosis drove this woman to seek psychoanalytic treatment. Both dreams also reveal conflicts within the treatment and with affective transference.

The following dream stems from transference conflicts [FIGURE 13].

4] *I am wearing red pajamas, ready for bed. I am going to take a bath, and to protect my head I am wearing a red rubber cap. I want to adjust my cap but it is too large and is coming to pieces. It is no good to me. I shall have to return it.*

Examining her associations, the patient was able to interpret the dream by herself. According to the patient, the red pajamas represented her love for the analyst, and her wish to go to bed, her desire to have a psychoanalytic session. The treatment itself was represented by having a bath, which meant cleansing herself of unpleasant dirt—her neurotic symptoms.

In the dream she wears a red rubber cap to protect her head. This signifies that to protect herself from her love troubles she has taken refuge in her love for the analyst. As we have pointed out, this love, which in psychoanalysis we call *positive transference,* must be analyzed and traced to its roots in childhood, the same as any other symptom.

Continuing her interpretation, the patient added: "*I want to adjust my cap:* I want to adapt the cap to my head. I want to adapt the doctor to myself, to make him love me as I love him, or *adapt my head to the cap,* adapt myself to reality. *But it is too large* [the cap]. The doctor is too big for me. He is not for me. *Moreover, it is coming to pieces* [the cap]. Moreover, he is detached from me. *It is no good to me* [the cap]. He is no good to me, he does not satisfy my love. *I shall have to return it* [the cap]. I shall have to give him up, because what I am feeling is transference."

Briefly, the interpretation reveals the woman's conflict about her need to understand that her love for the analyst was a transference reaction, that it was something that needed to be analyzed and could not be satisfied in reality. A daytime residue which gave the dream its special form was the fear that a contraceptive device had failed because the rubber had torn. In the manifest content of the dream, the dreamer, identifying herself with a man, puts on a rubber cap which afterwards appears torn. The rejection of her love by the analyst means not having become pregnant, for in the dream she puts on a pair of red pajamas, symbolizing the onset of her anxiously awaited menstruation.

5] [*The bird of paradise,* FIGURE 14.] *I am in my bedroom, lying down. I look up at the ceiling. I can see cobwebs and a strange object. I call the maid's attention to her carelessness and ask her to take away what I see. She brings a lance, spears the object, and brings it down. We look at it. It is a very white bird of paradise. It is dead.*

This dream is also connected with psychoanalytic treatment and the analyst. Part of the form of the dream came from the fact that on the morning before the dream the patient had met a foreigner wearing a bird-of-paradise feather on her hat. She had thought at the time that such feathers should not be worn in the morning but only later in the day when it was fashionable to wear smarter hats.

The patient continued her associations by saying that the ceiling (an analogy with the flat roof) symbolized her head, and that the word paradise awakened ideas of genital pleasure, reminding her of the expression "to be in paradise." She added that, living as she did at the time, "being in paradise" was something she had not experienced for a long time. Hence the bird of paradise is covered with cobwebs in the dream, like something which has been forgotten for a long time.

From these last associations we can deduce that lying down, as in previously related dreams, signified having psychoanalytic treatment. The analyst is represented by the maid—by someone who "serves" and helps her; he appears in the form of a woman because of the patient's genital repressions.

Spearing (or sticking on the end of a fork, as in a later dream) represents the psychoanalytic task of searching for whatever is to be found on the ceiling, i.e., in the head; in other words, investigating her thoughts, and these thoughts refer to the possibility of awakening her genitality which she considers dead, like the bird of paradise in the dream.

This is a superficial interpretation which can be complemented by considering the dreamer's associations to another dream element: the whiteness of the bird of paradise. It reminded her of leucorrhea, which her gynecologist had diagnosed some time previously. At that time she thought, and rightly so, that this leucorrhea was probably due to lack of genital satisfaction.

Continuing her train of associations, she said that her leucorrhea must surely come from the base of the vaginal sack. She further deduced that in the dream, therefore, the angle of the ceiling where the bird of paradise was stuck represented the base of her vaginal sack, and that its whiteness was an allusion to the leucorrhea. The act of spearing it with a lance (obviously a phallic symbol) indicated intercourse with the maid, i.e., the analyst. Thus we find at the basis of the dream a fantasy of intercourse with the analyst.

With this deep interpretation we can understand the latent meaning of her observation referring to what she had seen the day before, with which she began her associations. She had said that on the day before the dream she had seen a lady wearing a hat trimmed with a bird-of-paradise feather. She then remarked that such a hat should not be worn in the morning but only in the afternoon or evening. Knowing that her psychoanalytic session was in the morning, she unconsciously wished to convey that her desire for genital satisfaction—paradise—was not something that she should "wear" or feel in the morning; she should not make the analyst, whom she saw every morning, the object of her wishes.

She had thus rejected her transference wishes. During the day they had been pushed into the unconscious, but during the night, when her ego slept, the rejected wishes achieved expression in her dream, though in a disguised form. This is a regular occurrence in the formation of dreams, which always issue from rejected wishes due to the ego's reduced alertness during sleep.

(The manifest content of the dream also suggests the idea of an induced abortion. The bird of paradise would be the fetus; the cobwebs surrounding it, the fetal membranes; and the act of spearing, the scraping of the uterus. However, there was nothing in the patient's associations to indicate this interpretation.)

The following dream (which the woman did not draw) is similar to the previous one:

6] *The ceiling of the corridor in my home is not smooth in the dream. It is full of cobwebs with mosquitoes. I call the new maid and she tells me the last maid was careless with the cleaning because she knew she was leaving.*

In this dream, as frequently in other women's dreams, the corridor of the house represents the vagina. The ceiling, as in the previous dream, is again the upper part of the vagina; it is irregular in shape. The cobwebs indicate lack of sexual relations, whereas the mosquitoes, which bite, represent genital excitation. Lastly, the former maid, who has left, is her husband from whom she is separated, and the new maid is the analyst whom she consults about her troubles.

7] [*Red and yellow,* FIGURE 15.] *Someone shows me a drawing of a Scotch plaid painted in red and yellow. It is on a paper of copybook size. I have it in front of my eyes and do not see anything else. Between parallel and crossed straight lines there is, alternately, red and yellow. It is all enclosed in a yellow frame.*

Positive transference was at the bottom of this dream, which shows the analyst endowed with a series of good qualities. The patient herself interpreted this dream. In the following explanation only her own associations and conclusions are given.

She begins by talking about the red and yellow which are the colors of the Spanish flag, the country from which the analyst comes, and according to her, this is what the colors in the dream mean to her.

There are several reasons why the drawing should be of a tartan. First, Scotch implies foreign, and the analyst *is* foreign. The drawing is crisscrossed by long fine lines representing the analyst's height and slender appearance. Red stands for the analyst's tenderness and affection for her. She goes on to say that it is the tenderness and affection that all doctors have when they are interested in the well-being of their patients. Moreover, she adds, it is a projection onto the analyst of what she feels for him as a consequence of her affective transference.

Yellow she associates with the color of the analyst's skin, which she finds slightly sallow. It is a cold color, which reminds her of what she regards as a "cool and aloof attitude the analyst must adopt in order to treat his patients properly."

Altogether, the red and yellow spaces represent tenderness and seriousness, everything crossed by fine red lines which symbolize rectitude, manly goodness, and love.

And everything is surrounded by a yellow frame which is associated with the serious demeanor of the analyst and with his usual "cold *yellow* greeting" which, according to her, is meant to stop her transference feelings. On a deeper psychological level, and due to a play on words commonly used in Argentina, "Scotch" clearly implies genital wishes.

Lastly, her "not being able to see anything but the drawing" means that at that moment nothing exists for her but the analyst, because, she added, "it depends on him whether I obtain happiness in the future, once my psychological conflicts are overcome."

Among the unimportant residues of daytime occurrences, which the latent desires of her transference utilized in forming the manifest content of her dream, we find the following: On the days preceding the dream, the patient had explained straight and perpendicular lines to a geometry class. (In the dream the lines are crossed.) Some pupils drew those lines in yellow, but she advised them to draw them in red pencil because yellow is a pale, cold, and rather disagreeable color. She told them that red would put more life into their drawing.

The description and interpretation of the dream reveal how this daytime residue gave rise to the manifest content of the dream. Resuming the interpretation, it can be said that in this dream, through transference, based on a daytime residue, the analyst appears endowed with a series of good qualities. But this is not always the case; indeed, the very opposite is often true. For instance, in the following dream the analyst is represented by a madman:

8] [*The madman who was fishing,* FIGURE 16.] *I saw a large colonial patio. In the background there was a well. In the center, front, a madman was sitting on a low chair with a big basin of water on his knees. White, mud-colored, and red fish are swimming about restlessly. The madman catches them by sticking a fork into them, and he transfers them to another smaller basin on his right, on another low backless chair. Just at that moment he catches a very white fish. I am surprised that he catches them with a fork. I fear such treatment will hurt them, but it does not. He puts them into the smaller basin and they go on swimming about just as lively as ever. Nevertheless, it is not this basin which is worrying me but the other one.*

One of the daytime residues in this dream was a conversation the dreamer had had the day before with a very neurotic man about her psychoanalytic treatment. This man told her, among other things, that she would end up insane. But as she was aware of certain details of this man's life which were not normal, she thought that he would be more likely to end up insane than she.

These were her first associations, and on the basis of them she believed at first that the madman of the dream must be the man she had spoken with; but later associations showed her that the madman represented the analyst.

In fact, after the conversation we have just mentioned, she began to have associations with the colonial patio, which according to her was a Spanish patio and therefore related to the analyst. Then she chose as a new element for association the different-colored fish and thought they must refer to different kinds of thoughts. Her words were, "Ideas are like fish, which move about and escape from you." Further associations emerged from the element of changing fish from one basin to another. She associated this to ideas that had changed from unconscious to conscious ones—the object of her psychoanalytic sessions.

Later she insisted even more strongly on these associations and reiterated that the different-colored fish represented her different thoughts. Thus the white ones were her cheerful thoughts, the mud-colored ones her dirty thoughts, and the red ones, which are restless, her genital thoughts. The big basin is the unconscious mind and the small basin, the conscious. The different size is due to the fact that the unconscious is greater than the conscious. Finally, the madman spearing the fish represents the analyst, who tries to "fish" for unconscious ideas and turn them into conscious thoughts. The use of the term "fishing with a fork" for this activity is a gibe at the analyst.

"The basin is between the madman's legs" is, according to the patient, related to her impression that her head is between the analyst's legs when he sits behind her during the session.

In the dream, the patient fears that the procedure of fishing for her thoughts may hurt her, that psychoanalysis may produce anxiety. She must rid herself of repressions which, according to childhood beliefs, may bring unpleasant consequences; but the experience of past sessions, when she learned that this was not a problem, opposes this anguish; and the thoughts (or the fish in the dream) go on swimming around just as lively as ever, even after having been caught. Thus she says that it is not the small basin that worries her but the big one. In other words, she is not worried about the thoughts that are already conscious but only about those that are still unconscious.

"The madman is sitting on a low chair." As in many other dreams, something low represents sexuality, just as "low countries" in a dream can mean genital organs. This element of the dream must therefore mean that the analyst is concerned about her sexual thoughts.

The fact that the chair in the dream has no back, she associates with a pleasant impression: she thinks that during her sessions the analyst does not lean back in his armchair but leans toward her. The shadow projected on the wall proves this. Both her impression and the sensation of pleasure are due to her positive transference.

She reacts to her dissatisfaction and environmental submission by making fun of the analyst: this is why he appears as a madman in the dream. The well in the garden is a known symbol for the female genitals; in the dream the madman "has his back to it," meaning that he pays no attention to the well, that he is not interested in her as a woman but only in "fishing," in making her thoughts conscious. This activity, according to the patient's ideas, which up to then had been unconscious, is the behavior of a madman rather than that of a normal person.

9] *In a room there is a bed made up on the floor. I am waiting for my maid with whom I shall sleep. I go out to meet her but prefer to see a display of lights which has been installed in the street.*

The first part of the dream represents the psychoanalytic session, as can easily be seen from the drawing which the patient made of her dream [FIGURE 17]. The bed has the shape of the couch upon which she lies during her daily treatment, and the chandelier, too, looks like the one in the doctor's office. The servant, as in the previous dream of the bird of paradise, is the analyst who "serves" her by analyzing her conflicts, and by whom she is attracted because of her positive transference, and repelled because of her negative transference. (On another psychological plane, this part refers to her husband, for in her dream the room is her own.)

In the second part of the dream she easily gives up the analyst and prefers to see something outside psychoanalysis, which, even without the patient's associations and simply by her drawing, can be recognized as a symbol of the male genital organ ejaculating.

Briefly, in this dream her libidinal demands are adapted to reality. She solves her transference by withdrawing her libido from the analyst and directing it elsewhere, seeking adequate sexual satisfaction more or less consciously as a normal woman.

Chapter 2

THE DREAM WORK

In explaining the theory of dreams we can describe the various processes which play a part in their elaboration, factors which make the *latent content*—also called dream thoughts or latent thoughts—turn into *manifest content*, or the dream as the patient tells it.

Up to now we have been engaged in discovering, through interpretation, the latent thoughts behind the manifest content. Now we shall do the opposite, and starting from latent thoughts we shall see how they are transformed into manifest content, into dream images.

The easiest dreams to understand are those called infantile dreams. They are usually dreams that satisfy organic desires or needs, such as hunger, thirst, or excremental needs. A person is uncomfortable because of an organic need and dreams of satisfying that need. He is thirsty, for example, and he dreams that he is drinking; the psychological force that leads to the formation of the dream is the desire to drink. In sleep the person has a thought such as "I want a drink." In the dream he sees himself drinking because the latent wish has been converted into an optical image. This is perhaps the essence of transformation in the elaboration of dreams: the conversion of latent thoughts into *concrete images*. We could express this in another way by saying that, in the waking state, instinctual impulses lead to thoughts and actions, and during sleep they lead to latent thoughts which are transformed into the images of the manifest dream.

In view of the fact that dream images do not correspond to material realities, these images may be described as hallucinatory. Thus during the formation of the dream the latent thoughts are converted into hallucinatory images. One must bear this transformation in mind when interpreting the dream. For instance, in the theoretical case of an undistorted dream (supposing that such a dream could exist) in which the dreamer is drinking, the interpretation consists of stating that the dreamer wanted to drink. The image of the dream must be interpreted in terms of latent wishes.

We apply the term *distortion of dreams* to the transformations which latent thoughts undergo before they appear in the manifest content. These transformations include condensation, displacement, symbolization, and secondary revision.

In order to affirm or deny the existence of distortion in dreams, it is not enough to observe the manifest content and deduce from it whether the dream is comprehensible. Some dreams may seem perfectly understandable, but their latent meaning may differ completely from that appearing in the manifest content.

Through *condensation,* various latent thoughts appear represented in a single element of the manifest content. Thus, for instance, four people, A, B, C, and D, of the latent content, appear in the manifest content as only one person. But this person has some characteristics of A, dresses like B, has C's mannerisms, and lives in D's house; thus he represents four separate people in the latent content. (The comic strip in FIGURE 18 illustrates this graphically.)

In the dream work all, or nearly all, dreams go through a process of condensation. The dream work usually collects many latent thoughts, seeks analogies and points of contact among these thoughts, and through these forms a condensed dream. Condensation also explains why dreams are generally short.

The contrary of condensation is the splitting of elements, in which a person or object in the latent thoughts corresponds to two or more elements in the manifest content, thus representing different characteristics of the single latent element. For example, different feelings of the dreamer may be represented by different persons in the manifest dream.

Displacement is another mechanism frequently used in the dream work. Owing to displacement, latent thoughts appear in the manifest content not as they are but only in part, or in the form of allusions. (This kind of representation is known technically as synecdoche or metonymy.) Another form of displacement in the dream work consists in emphasizing something in the manifest content which in latent thoughts is only of secondary value, while the most important element takes a secondary place.

Displacement is the most important process in dream distortion. No other psychological factor contributes as much to making dreams incomprehensible.

Displacement also occurs commonly in everyday life, for reasons analogous to those in dreams. When speaking of ugly people we say that they are lacking in grace, or that they are nice; of old people, that they are getting on in years; of a stupid person, that he is absent-minded; of people who steal, that they are attracted to other people's property; and so on. And there are a number of euphemisms that are used in speaking about sex, so that no direct mention of the subject need be made.

Symbolization, which may be considered a special form of displacement, is another of the processes that intervene in the dream work. When a particular concrete element of the manifest content is related with some constancy in different dreams to a repressed element of the latent content, it is called a symbol.

The psychoanalytic concept of symbols is more limited than the general one. For a concrete element of the manifest content of a dream to be considered a symbol, the thing which is symbolized must have been repressed. In everyday language, however, a scale symbolizes justice; a flag, patriotism; a handclasp, friendship; a triangle and plumbline, Freemasonry; a serpent, medicine; a crown, royalty; and so on. We find similar symbols in art; in one of Goya's etchings, for instance [FIGURE

19], lies are symbolized by two faces, and inconstancy by butterfly wings on a woman's head.

Very few psychoanalytic assertions have been so criticized, both by educated and ignorant people, as those referring to symbolism. Nevertheless, its validity has been most frequently confirmed, and without any great effort. Every day we receive data from patients' dreams which prove the point.

Moreover, psychoanalysis has shown that the existence and meaning of symbols can be proven experimentally. A demonstration was given by Schroetter as far back as 1912. He induced deep hypnosis in his experimental subjects and then ordered them to have a dream about a specific sexual matter that was unpleasant to them. The hypnotized person obeyed this order, but in the dream the unpleasant content was symbolized. For instance, a woman who was told to dream of having sexual relations with another woman, had a dream in which she saw a valise with the inscription "For ladies only." A valise was already known to be a female genital symbol.

Betlheim and Hartmann made a similar experiment in 1924 on patients with Korsakoff's syndrome. They told their patients little stories with openly sexual content and then asked them to repeat the stories. In the patients' versions the stories were distorted through symbolization. They used symbols such as "going up a flight of stairs," with a latent meaning of coitus, which could not be considered *conscious* distortions of material. For example, one story described in a vulgar way the rape of a young woman by two men in the country. One of the patients retold it as follows: "Two girls were going up a flight of stairs. Two men were following them. One of them married one of the girls because she was pregnant. The other one went home." Another patient used the following symbolism: "He thrust the knife into the scabbard." A third patient spoke of a "cigarette" instead of the penis.

Leslie H. Farber and Charles Fisher, in 1943, also carried out research on symbols with hypnotized persons. They studied two distinct aspects, one concerning dream interpretation and the other the experimental production of dreams. They exposed the hypnotized subjects to stimuli connected with different situations, then ordered them to dream and tell their dreams. They tried to avoid stimuli which were especially traumatic, because otherwise they could not easily be elaborated into dreams. This technique allowed them to investigate the relationship between the dream symbols and the preceding stimuli and once again confirmed psychoanalytic investigations. Moreover, approximately 20 per cent of the hypnotized subjects were able to understand fully the dream symbols, although they had no notion of psychology or special talents for it in the waking state.

The presence of other people, besides the hypnotist, influenced the results of the experiments. For example, to the stimulus of having an unmarried and pregnant girl friend, a girl dreamed she was on a small island, surrounded by enormous waves and being heavily rained upon. When one of those present asked her what the dream meant, she answered conventionally, interpreting the island as social isolation and the rain as the censure a single woman with a child would have to suffer. But to the hypnotist she said that the rain represented semen. In other cases, the presence of a woman caused male subjects to have dreams symbolic of coitus, such as going through tunnels.

Even in modern language it is possible to demonstrate the existence of words with a double meaning, one sexual and the other asexual. The English word *staff* or the German *stab* come from the Germanic root *staber*, which means to stand upright. Three centuries ago the word *yard* meant both stick and penis. The same is true of the French word *verge*. The German word *Zimmer* means room, while colloquially a woman is called *Frauenzimmer* (literally, woman-room). *Coger* in Argentina means both to pick up and to copulate, although in Spain and some other Spanish-speaking countries it has no conscious sexual meaning.

Those who object to the theory of symbolism claim that if there are connections between the symbols and what is symbolized, then, conversely, what is symbolized should also be capable of representing the symbol. For example, if the stick is frequently used as a symbol for the penis, why should not the penis be a frequent symbol for the stick? It is not difficult to refute this objection: the idea of a stick is not repressed and need not be expressed symbolically.

Apart from linguistic connections between symbols and what is symbolized, it is important to know that symbols do not appear only in dreams but also in other psychological activities, such as in mythology, rituals, folklore, jokes, literature, and proverbs.

An example of symbolism in decorative art is the various ways in which the feline motive is represented by the Diaguite Indians [FIGURE 20]. The tiger and leopard symbolize the castrating father or the pre-oedipal, devouring mother. In order to avoid the disagreeable psychological tensions evoked by the feared parents, they are replaced by an animal that takes on a totemic aspect. However, the anxiety is only partially alleviated by this process, and the representation of the parent substitute is disguised more and more until it becomes practically unrecognizable. The techniques used are strange and varied—for example, the use of duplication and multiplication, which are also present in dreams.

In dreams, as well as in mythology or art, symbols are created to conceal thoughts repressed by the censorship of the ego. Unconscious wishes, the ego, and the super-ego (or conscience) reflect the outer world and play a role in the genesis of symbols. Since these factors depend on dynamic forces, their product—symbols—are subject to vicissitudes, depending on their respective strengths. This may be demonstrated concretely in a different area of human activity, namely advertising.

A certain perfume manufacturer advertises one of his products with pictures showing two musicians [FIGURE 21]. We know from psychoanalytic experience that the playing of musical instruments in dreams usually represents sexual activity. This interpretation may be given to this picture, especially when the kiss between the characters leaves little doubt as to their desires. This interpretation is borne out when we see the antecedents of the picture. I found one of them in a painting by Louis Boilly, "Prelude to Nina," painted about 1780 [FIGURE 22]. The theme and symbols are identical, but they are portrayed in such a manner that the latent content is much less masked. The meaning of the violin is very clear, particularly in view of its position in the man's pubic region, its direction, and the way it is fondled by the woman. With this interpretation as a springboard, it is easy to interpret the piano as the female genital organ. Therefore, what is symbolized is a mutual genital caress which corresponds to the other elements of the characters' attitude, the room in which they find themselves, and, above all, the title of the painting, "Prelude to Nina"—prelude having the double meaning of a genital introduction and of a piece of music.

In both graphic and literary art, hidden contents are symbolically repeated several times. In the painting in FIGURE 22 we see the walking stick, near the man, as a phallic symbol, and a guitar next to the woman, with the feminine opening clearly visible. Similarly, the paper next to the guitar is a female symbol, corresponding to the overcoat, a male symbol, opposite. The meaning is repeated by the piano stool and the armchair, one of them having a high back and the other none, alluding to unconscious concepts of the female genital organ having suffered phallic castration. This picture was painted in the years preceding the French Revolution, when morals in France were very free. The perfume advertisers, in using the same theme, had to modify the picture in order to disguise its meaning. Although the general situation remains the same, each character plays his own instrument in the present picture and stands in such a way as not to expose the latent content quite so clearly. It shows, nevertheless, a loving posture which makes the sexual excitement of the woman evident and symbolizes the man's erection by his raised arm, holding the violin. The other sexual symbols have disappeared from this picture because the repression is greater, and the bed, which may be behind the door, is modestly hidden by a curtain. On the other hand, evening dress appears as a new symbol of these hidden contents. The advertisers explain that the name of the perfume, "Tabu," is synonomous with "prohibited." Psychoanalytically we know that what is prohibited is intimately connected with sexuality. This explains the search for an exciting picture to attract customers; the name of the perfume and the advertisement act jointly in creating identical situations.

The attenuation of contents between eighteenth- and twentieth-century painting is the result of a most energetic repression. There is more prudishness in modern times. This is so true that even the picture in question seems too audacious and because of unconscious insinuations must be further disguised. This is what happens in the later editions of the advertisement [FIGURES 23 and 24]. In one of them the characters lack the vitality of the preceding picture, and although they are actually there, they seem to be far away and shadowy, as if imperceptible and unreal; they symbolize sexual desires that have given way before repression. That they are old-fashioned characters replaced by modern people indicates something which existed in the past but has changed by being subjected to repression.

In FIGURE 24 repression works in such a way that the symbolization by musical instruments disappears and is replaced in the man by the symbol of the overcoat. Apart from the kiss, the sexual excitement is indicated by the posture, especially of the woman. The bright coloring and the presence of flowers also point to erotic feelings.

In these advertisements the repression of sexual content is intense—so intense that what is repressed tends to burst forth into the open. This has been perceived by a caricaturist who pokes fun at the theme [FIGURE 25] by making the woman protest against the grandiose but sterile gestures of the man and demand direct satisfaction. A further confirmation of repression is the fact that the advertisers found themselves in a similar psychological situation. Indeed, in the last of the advertisements [FIGURE 26] it is clear that the characters have directly sought instinctual pleasure. There is no one to be seen in the picture; obviously they are doing something which is not for the public eye. But we see the fallen piano stool and the fallen bow of the violin which, in the general situation of the painting and in the light of the preceding pictures, are clear symbols of full sexual surrender, of lying down.

Continuing with an explanation of symbolism in general, it is interesting to note that when we ask a person what he thinks about the symbolic elements of his dream, his associations often fail and he thinks of nothing at all. For this reason Freud called symbols "the dumb elements of dreams." To interpret their meaning, material from other psychological manifestations, such as folklore or literature, may be used.

In dreams, or in the psychological manifestations just mentioned, there is a very constant relation between the symbol and its meaning. But this does not imply that a symbol cannot have more than one meaning, or that its meaning is invariable; on the contrary, its presence and meaning sometimes vary in accordance with cultural environment, but the variation is small.

Whereas the number of symbols is large, the number of ideas symbolically represented in dreams is limited. There are possibly not more than a hundred such thoughts, referring mostly to sexuality, birth, death, the dreamer himself, and his nearest relatives. (See at the end of the book the lists of symbols and of things symbolized.)

Emperors, kings, military or political chiefs, governors, teachers, bosses, and generally all persons with authority symbolize parents. Schoolmates, workmates, professional and sporting associates, and, generally, people whose activities are similar to those of the dreamer represent his siblings. Siblings are also symbolized by insects, such as worms, bugs, and fleas. Houses represent people, but houses with protruding balconies symbolize women, and houses with flat façades symbolize men. Scenery, according to its contour, may also represent the human body, male or female.

Birth is usually symbolized by placing a person near water —either putting him into water or taking him out and saving him from drowning.

Elongated objects, such as pencils, cigarettes, walking sticks, umbrellas, skis, trees; or objects which bore holes or cause wounds, such as daggers, knives, sabres, spears, needles, bull's horns, toothpicks, files, firearms; objects which fit in a hole, such as keys; objects which eject things, such as hoses, fountains, petrol pumps, bellows [DREAM 1]; objects capable of rising or increasing in size, such as balloons, dirigibles, airplanes, kites;—all these objects symbolize the male genital organ. Other symbols for the male genital organ are items of clothing, such as hats, overcoats, and capes; animals, such as birds, fishes, reptiles, and, especially, snakes; human organs, such as eyes and, especially, teeth, and the head, the arm, the hand, and the foot; numbers, such as the number three. The testicles are symbolized by fruits or by words which sound the same as testicles; semen is symbolized by blood or by something valuable, such as money [DREAM 3].

Female genitals are symbolized by objects which are able to contain something or shelter someone, such as ships [DREAM 2], wardrobes, trunks, arks, drawers, boxes, bags, purses, ditches, caverns, caves, mines, basins, stoves, ovens. A room is a symbol for the woman's belly or genital organs, although it may also have other meanings. The female genitals are also symbolized by the earth, wood, paper, a table, a book, a flower. Fruits are another female symbol, and so are the mouth and the ear. Clothes which symbolize the female are boots, shoes, and slippers; animals such as snails and mussels also symbolize women, and so does the number two. The vulva and the vagina are often symbolized by a fissure, a diamond or oval shape, the entrance to a cave, a church, chapel, porch, door, or window. The breasts are symbolized by rounded fruits, such as apples or peaches, while the banana is a male symbol. The *mons veneris* is symbolized by a forest, a garden, or a railing [DREAM 1]. A younger brother or a child represents genital organs, both male and female. In general, all symbols can have male or female meanings.

Flying or rising symbolizes erection, in the same way as going down is related to the position of the genitals low in the body [DREAM 8]. Falling, being trampled on, or stumbling may symbolize a woman's surrender to a man. Fire may symbolize sexual excitement, and so may the color red [DREAM 4], the presence of animals and savages, mythological beings, mad people, or sick people. Coitus is symbolized through rhythmic movements, such as going up and coming down stairs, sweeping chimneys, dancing, riding horseback, and swaying [DREAM 2]; also by eating, smoking, or playing some musical instrument. Generally, any activity can symbolize sexual activity: to go on board [DREAM 2], to ride in a car, to walk in the street, to grab, to enter, to spear [DREAM 5], to go for a walk, to wed, to go to the theater, to telephone.

Ernest Jones, Otto Rank, and Hanns Sachs have made the most thorough study of symbolism. We can affirm, as they do, that if symbolic meanings of a sexual order predominate it is because no other instinct is so subject to pressure by social conventions and so frequently deprived of direct satisfaction. Moreover, the sexual instinct is composed of multiple and varied "perverse" elements which undergo intense repression and so are liable to find symbolic representation. Finally, it is interesting to note that ancient civilizations placed great importance on the genital organs and their functions. This may seem monstrous to us today, but the fact has been clearly demonstrated by ethnological research and by traces left in myths and primitive cults.

Briefly, the characteristics of symbolism, in the psychoanalytic sense, may be summed up as follows: a connection with unconscious processes; a meaning which is practically constant and frequently sexual; independence from individual factors; linguistic connections; and the existence of similar symbols in various other manifestations of the human psyche.

What other transformations intervene in the formation of the manifest dream content? So far we have considered condensation, displacement, and symbolization. There is one other process in dream work known as *secondary revision,* or elaboration, which perfects the dream from the conscious point of view. In ordinary terms, it may be said that secondary revision puts the last touches to a dream, making it more precise and more comprehensible in its formal aspect.

Secondary revision may be likened to the process that converts our perceptions into representations. Suppose, for instance, that we have a cube before us. We perceive only three of its sides but deduce nevertheless that there must be three more sides; we imagine these three hidden sides, which together with the visible ones give us the representation of a cube. Therefore, something we cannot perceive we imagine through secondary revision, which synthesizes our perceptions with the help of memories of former perceptions. Secondary revision also contributes to the perception of movement in the movies, because when we look at consecutive images of a body in different positions, we suppose it has moved from one position to another.

Secondary revision sometimes causes errors in perception. This happens, for instance, when we fail to perceive a printer's error while reading a book; the printer's error would alter the entire harmony of our reading, and so we eliminate it. Secondary revision also occurs when an audience observes the manipulations of a magician.

In dreams, secondary revision tries to create a harmonious manifest content without contradictions. Its activity is sometimes easy to see. For example, the following dream: "I am going to the notary, or rather, he comes to my house and looks at everything I have." The words "or rather" are added because of secondary revision. In fact, the interpretation shows that the notary is the psychoanalyst, that the dreamer himself is symbolized by his home and the psychoanalytic exploration by the notary's act of entering his home. Thus this quotation from the dream means: "I am going to the psychoanalyst's office, and he will explore my mind." Without the secondary revision, the dream would have had the following manifest content: "I am going to the notary's office and he comes to my home." Thus two apparently contradictory actions would appear in the manifest content. The introduction of "or rather" destroys the contradiction and gives the dream a more logical aspect. In DREAM 2 secondary revision caused the dreamer to change the graphic representation of her dream [FIGURES 11 AND 12].

In the manifest dream content, the additions introduced by secondary revision lend the dream a more coherent character; at the same time, however, the dream loses some perceptive vitality. The dreamer seldom has associations relating to the revised elements, which are the first to be forgotten.

A person is apt to react to his dreams with a sense of strangeness, which rarely happens with regard to other psychological phenomena. This sensation, connected with something that comes from the subject himself, is very rare in psychological life. Generally a person recognizes as his own what he thinks, does, or imagines. Even in certain cases where something psychological is not his own, he still assimilates it to his ego. The most typical example of this tendency is the one known as the post-hypnotic mandate. A person is hypnotized and asked to perform some act after waking—for instance, he is asked to open a window in the room five minutes after he awakes. On awakening he carries out the order faithfully but has no memory of what happened when he was hypnotized and therefore does not know the reason for his action. But on being asked why he opened the window, he always finds, without being aware of it, a reason which he firmly believes. Thus he answers, for example, that he opened the window because the room was too warm. He thinks that the action is his own idea and is not aware that the motivation is external.

The very opposite occurs in dreams. The subject is aware of the fact that he has produced the dream, and yet it feels strange to him. It is this sense of strangeness which suggested to people in ancient times that dreams came from the beyond.

Most dreams in adults are incomprehensible to the dreamer. Moreover, if the interpretation the dreamer gives to his dream is examined, it is usually found to be incorrect. But the sensation of strangeness which the dream produces is only partly due to the lack of comprehension. It is only in part, too, the result of condensation, displacement, and symbolism. The sense of strangeness derives mostly from the fact that the latent thoughts which give rise to the dream are thoughts that the dreamer does not wish to acknowledge as his own. A dream generally masks latent thoughts which are unpleasant to the ego. Certain latent thoughts capable of giving rise to dreams reach the manifest content; others do not. We may suppose that there is a psychological force, somewhere between the latent thoughts and the manifest contents, which makes a selection. Psychoanalysis has called the force *censorship.* The dream censorship permits only the passage of those thoughts which fulfill a series of conditions and thereby become acceptable to the ego.

Rejected thoughts endeavor to, and actually do, come through, but they are distorted by displacement and symbolization. This distortion of thoughts, stemming from instinctual life, is also operative in the origin of neuroses. Thus the genesis of dreams shows great similarity to the genesis of neurotic symptoms, and a therapist who cannot understand dreams cannot hope to understand the intricate psychological mechanisms of neuroses.

Latent thoughts are permitted to pass into the manifest content only if they are acceptable to the dreamer's own morality and his unconscious super-ego. Certain thoughts, which are immoral from the collective point of view, are often tolerated perfectly well by a person, while others, which from a social point of view are innocent, may provoke intense remorse in him. When interpreting dreams we must try to discover the dreamer's particular norm of morals. Expressed in psychoanalytic terms, we must try to discover the special characteristics of the dreamer's super-ego by finding out which thoughts are rejected by the dream censorship, because the dream censorship is a manifestation of the super-ego.

Transformation into concrete images, condensation, displacement, symbolization, and secondary revision are responsible for the conversion of latent thoughts into the dream proper. But what are latent thoughts and where do they come from? Their character is easy to define. There is no difference between the latent thoughts that give rise to a dream and those we have in our waking state. Knowing this, one can understand the variety of latent thoughts. Thoughts which enter into a dream may come from a fantasy, a judgment, a memory, a desire, a political idea, an attempt to solve a conflict, something which has to be done, a painful experience, an ambition or resentment, charitable purposes or criminal thoughts, and so on. They may be sexual thoughts or not at all connected with sexuality. To assert that only sexual desires intervene in dreams would be erroneous and completely alien to psychoanalysis.

In spite of their changeability, latent thoughts are *always important thoughts*. Only important thoughts can motivate a dream, although the trivial is exactly what appears in the manifest content.

Latent thoughts are products of mental activity which continues during sleep. The fact that this activity is unconscious does not disprove its existence. Who, for example, will deny the possibilities of mental conflicts being solved during sleep? A solution seems clear when one wakes the following morning, even though the night before everything had seemed confused.

In the manifest dream content, elements appear that proceed from the events of the day preceding the dream. Freud called these elements *day residues*. There are day residues which have not been consciously perceived, and, nevertheless, later form part of a dream. The following experiment shows this clearly. Poetzl showed images very rapidly to different people by means of a tachistoscope and afterwards asked the subjects to draw in detail what they had seen. He could thus verify which details had not been noticed. The next day he would ask these same subjects to draw their dreams of the night before, and he frequently observed that in these drawings patients included elements of the images which had not been consciously perceived, since they had not drawn them on the first occasion. Although these elements had not been consciously perceived, they formed part of the manifest content of the dream.

Many day residues which appear in the manifest content are not important. One may say that a dream, or the manifest content of a dream, prefers something recent and unimportant, but the unimportant detail is associated with important things, and because of this association it forms part of the dream. The unimportant detail is not an activating element in itself; it is always included in the manifest dream content because of a displacement.

It is easy to understand that the manifest content of a dream should choose something recent and unimportant to represent important latent thoughts which have been rejected by censorship. The form of recent important memories is too precisely determined by its connections, by its important feelings and thoughts, to be able to represent other, equally important thoughts. On the other hand, recent trivial details can easily enter into mental associations which modify and join their meaning to important repressed ideas.

A dream utilizes recent events in preference to childhood events. But dreams also show the imprint of childhood experiences. This is evident in the analysis of dreams, in which thoughts related to childhood experiences, often *consciously* forgotten, are frequently found. But there is a difference in the way recent and childhood experiences are presented; recent happenings seek the manifest content, but childhood experiences are to be found in latent thoughts and are represented in the manifest content only through allusions. The importance of childhood experiences in dreams is so great that Freud ventures the hypothesis that all dreams have two distinct sources: the present and childhood.

Unconscious wishes are another factor which regularly intervenes in the genesis of dreams. These wishes are often repressed, of an infantile nature, and unacceptable by adult moral standards.

Two factors contribute to all adult dreams: latent thoughts

and unconscious wishes. According to Freud, a dream is always a hallucinatory fulfillment (distorted) of an unconscious wish (repressed), through latent thoughts. One of these factors alone cannot produce a dream; the unconscious wish needs a representation through which it can express itself, and latent thoughts need the drive of unconscious wishes.

This combination is the most complicated part of dream psychology, and it is difficult to understand clearly. It would be easier to explain the genesis of dreams if only one of these factors were involved. But dreams, like other psychological phenomena, are not as simple to explain as we would like them to be. Therefore we must adjust ourselves to their complexity and avoid erroneous simplifications which hide the essence of the phenomenon.

Freud explains the existing relationship between latent thoughts and unconscious wishes by a comparison: A dream is like a business that has two partners, the industrialist who supplies the ideas of the business, and the capitalist; each partner needs the other. In dreams, latent thoughts would be the industrial partner, and the unconscious wish the capitalist. The problem becomes complicated, both in business and in dreams, because the industrial partner sometimes also has a small capital, and the capitalist may have some interesting ideas to offer. Sometimes there are several industrial partners and only one capitalist, or vice versa. One must always bear these complications in mind, because psychological phenomena, like biological or financial ones, are not all adaptable to the same pattern.

Unconscious desires and latent thoughts are the material used by dreams, as well as the basis of their formation. The dreamer's wish to sleep is another factor, since the dreamer does not wish to awaken. There are dreams in which this wish to sleep appears very clearly, and these are commonly called *dreams of convenience*. In them the dreamer performs a task which he should be doing in reality. This is the case with a person who is called out of bed in the morning and dreams he is already at work doing his daily job. It is easy to find the meaning of the dream; the dreamer has two conflicting tendencies: one, his sense of duty which urges him to get up, and the other, his wish to take advantage of the comfort he is enjoying. The dream satisfies both tendencies: the dreamer continues to sleep but dreams he is performing his job.

The same thing happens in dreams which satisfy organic needs, such as hunger or thirst. The dreamer finds himself tormented by his organic need; he would have to wake up and perform a series of motions to attain his end; instead, he dreams, and this allows him to continue sleeping while his need is satisfied by hallucination.

As the satisfaction afforded by the dream is only hallucinatory, and not real, it often happens that ultimately the dream cannot fulfill the need, and the dreamer is finally forced by his organic need to wake up. But this is not always the case; some dreams do give real satisfaction. For instance, in the manifest content of dreams of sexual excitement, there are usually more or less disguised love scenes. If there is a nocturnal emission, the instinct is satisfied and the dreamer continues to sleep without dreams. This also happens in the dreams of enuretics, when they dream they are in a place suitable for urinating. If they wake up later, it is because of fears or secondary discomfort. But in both these types of dreams there are important unconscious desires which do not appear in the manifest content.

Without generalizing extensively it is possible to say that all dreams are dreams of convenience. Interruption of sleep may have various causes: some are of mental origin and others of physical origin. Among the former, there are, on the one hand, instinctual wishes clamoring for immediate satisfaction; and on the other hand, anxiety, often linked with the worry of projects, intentions, and problems that have not been solved during the day and which, when heavily charged affectively, do not permit sleep. Organic troubles, such as stomach ache, or external factors, such as an alarm clock, may of course also interrupt sleep.

Dreams attempt to pacify all these enemies of sleep. Organic discomfort is included in dreams in such a way that the dreamer deceives himself through an erroneous but convenient interpretation. Suppose a dreamer is suffering intestinal cramps; he may dream of an army crossing a narrow space, led by some soldiers playing the trumpet. The same happens with external stimuli: the sound of an alarm clock going off (as in the case of Hildebrandt in 1875) may be interpreted by the dreamer as the sound of church bells on a fine summer day, or as the bells on a Russian troika, in which a person travels wrapped up in heavy furs which give him comfortable warmth. Even in dreams caused by organic or external stimuli, the dreamer's psychological characteristics are present, for the stimulus is interpreted according to those characteristics. The stimulus is able to create a dream only as long as it is reflected in the latent thoughts and with the help of an unconscious desire. Psychologically, these dreams are not different from others, and their interpretation leads to the same results.

One of the most interesting experiments in the field of dream observation was undertaken in 1953 by Nathaniel Kleitman, professor of physiology in the University of Chicago, in collaboration with Eugene Asenirsky and later with William Dement. Their research was based on sporadic observations of the fact that during sleep people at times move their eyes very rapidly. They presumed that this was an indication of dreaming, and this was confirmed when the people were awakened at times when they were moving their eyes.

Kleitman then decided to investigate the sleeping and dreaming habits of people of different social levels and professions, who were paid to participate in the experiments. Electrodes were placed on the skin to record the movement of eyes and limbs, and also heartbeat and brain activity.

When the subjects were awakened during periods of rapid ocular movements, 80 per cent reported dreams, while only 6 per cent of those whose eyes were in repose reported dreams. Furthermore, the type of ocular movement was directly related to the type of dream. A subject whose ocular movements were vertical was dreaming that he was standing at the foot of a cliff, up which he could see people climbing, and that he himself was in charge of a crane. Another subject with similar eye movements reported a dream of catching basketballs and throwing them into the net above him. Another subject with horizontal eye movements reported a dream of watching two men engaged in a tennis match, but with tomatoes instead of tennis balls.

While the eyes may move rapidly during a dream, the rest of the body is immobile—although the contrary was usually supposed to be true. It is almost as though the subject makes himself comfortable in bed, as though he were in his seat at the theater, in order to watch the dream scene being enacted on his field of vision. As the experiments showed, it is only when the ocular movements cease that the subject modifies his position in bed.

Many actions in a dream take about the same time as they would in real life. This has been observed by comparing the duration of rapid ocular movements with the content of the dream. In order to measure this even more exactly, Kleitman's research workers occasionally made the subjects repeat in real life the actions they had dreamed.

It was possible to deduce from the electroencephalogram that dreams (indicated by rapid movements of the eyes) occur when sleep is less profound. The episodes of dreaming occur several times during the night, and there appear to be cycles in which deep, dreamless sleep alternates with light sleep, during which dreams occur. The average duration of each cycle appears to be about ninety minutes, and that of the rapid ocular movements lasts about twenty minutes. During the night there appear to be about five or six separate periods of dreaming which compose about 20 per cent of the total time of sleep. In other words, people probably have five or six dreams a night in spite of the fact that in the morning they may remember only one or two, or perhaps none at all. During the night, if the subject wakens even a few minutes after his rapid movements of the eyes have ceased, he has usually completely forgotten the dream which is presumed to have accompanied them.

In recent years Charles Fisher has been the analyst most actively engaged in experimental research into dreams. He has used the method of subliminal visual stimulation. Fisher began by repeating experiments previously carried out by Poetzl. He exposed pictures to various subjects for a hundredth of a second, then asked them to draw what they had seen. Those parts of the picture that they had not consciously perceived, and that therefore were not reproduced in their drawings, later appeared in the manifest contents of their dreams. In other words, they were *preconsciously* perceived and later appeared in the dreams as day residues.

In order to investigate the chronological relationship between external stimuli and dream processes, Fisher repeated the experiments in a slightly modified form. He again exposed a picture for a hundredth of a second, and the next day he administered word-association tests, in which he usually chose as stimulus words those which designated objects that had not been consciously perceived in the pictures. Sometimes he conducted these tests immediately after the pictures had been exposed, and sometimes two or three days later. In addition—and this is the most crucial part of the experiment—the subjects were requested to report and make a drawing of any images which developed in their minds in the time between hearing the stimulus word and giving their response word.

The unnoticed parts of the pictures appeared in these drawings in an almost photographic way, so that some of the subjects were able to attain an almost complete photographic reconstruction of the momentarily exposed picture.

For instance, a picture of two Siamese cats and a parakeet were exposed to a woman for a hundredth of a second. She did not notice the parakeet consciously; her first drawing was of two dog-like animals, which appeared to be a fusion of the cats and bird in the exposed picture. She later gave the response "mouse" to the stimulus word "cat." She became confused while doing a second drawing and remarked that in it the cat was more like a hawk chasing a bird. Her drawing was really a bird-like mammal.

The second stimulus word, "dog," elicited the response "house." She drew a watchdog, but this also resembled a bird. In her next drawing, the compulsive apparition of the bird image was much stronger: the animal she drew looked much less like a mammal than the cat she had previously drawn.

This picture of the two cats and the parakeet reactivated very deep-seated oral-sadistic material in all the persons to whom it was exposed, based on the idea that cats prey on birds. In several drawings there was a repetition of the theme of a bird or a child's head against the body of a cat. These drawings suggest that the persons taking part in the experiment were struggling with intense oral strivings, and that they were confused between activity and passivity, between mother and child, between male and female.

These experiments show that some of our conscious mental images are caused by the same evolutive process which gives rise to dream images.

Similar images appeared in combinations of the experiments, i.e., the drawing of dreams which occurred after pictures had been momentarily exposed, followed by the drawing of images arising from word association. These experiments clearly showed that the masking process, manifest in dreams, actually begins during the day, in fact as soon as a person perceives any content on which his unconscious psychic traumata or wishes act. This creates a memory trace of the masked, distorted percept, which later becomes even more distorted during the course of the day, before becoming part of the dream content. In the genesis of dreams, the images of wishes and traumata from the past, which motivate the dream, make contact with the recent memory images of the percepts connected with the day residue, some of which have already undergone distortion. These memory pictures from the past are covered by the recent memory images and give rise to the manifest content of the dream.

The results of these experiments suggest that perception, like any other mental activity, first goes through an unconscious phase before becoming conscious. This means that perception is not situated in the field of the conscious, as Freud described and pointed out in a drawing in his paper, "The Ego and the Id."

Chapter 3

DREAMS IN PSYCHOANALYTIC TREATMENT

Since dream interpretation and research are carried out during psychoanalytic treatment, it would be useful to explain some of the details of technique.

Dreams are easily forgotten. Dreams that are clearly remembered at the moment of awakening are frequently completely forgotten when the patient arrives for his analytic session. To avoid this the patient is sometimes advised to keep paper and pencil by his bedside and write down his dream as soon as he awakes.

But this is bad technique. In the first place, it is annoying for the patient to sleep while worrying about his dreams and knowing that he must write them down as soon as he awakes. Secondly, this technique in no way helps in the interpretation. When he writes out his dreams the patient only notes the manifest content, which, as we already know, is of little value unless accompanied by those latent thoughts that are only obtained through his associations. The dream that is written down on awakening loses some of its psychic connections during the day; but these connections explain its source, lead to the interpretation, and condition its being forgotten.

A dream is not forgotten because of its incoherence, but rather because of the influence of repressions which try to remove from consciousness elements with unpleasant latent meanings. This is shown by the fact that dreams that have already been interpreted and are, therefore, no longer incoherent, are often forgotten as easily as those which have not been interpreted. In both cases forgetting is a consequence of repression.

It is true that a dream that is written down on awakening is not forgotten, but often the associations relative to the dream are lacking when the dream comes to be interpreted. This in itself would not be a great inconvenience, since the analyst, through his knowledge of the patient's life and of the meaning of symbols, is sometimes able to understand the dream. But the therapeutic problem in neurosis does not consist in the analyst's knowledge of what the dreams mean; it is also necessary that the patient *understand* his dream. It is not enough for the analyst to tell him its meaning, since not only an intellectual understanding but a deep, affective one is indispensable for a positive therapeutic result. In interpretation the patient's associations establish connections between his conscious awareness and his repressed unconscious. The therapist's work can only be a help to, but never a substitute for, the patient's efforts.

The patient may say he has forgotten what he dreamed. Generally it is not totally forgotten, for fragments of the dream are often remembered later during the course of the session. But if this does not happen, the patient will soon have another dream which he will not forget and which will also, naturally, proceed from his repressed unconscious. Interpretation may begin with fragments of dreams or dreams that are totally remembered. Experience teaches us that very often what remains in the memory—the part of the dream that is not forgotten—is the easiest to interpret. This is not strange, because forgetting is conditioned by repression. In these cases, therefore, the partial forgetting of a dream is a help and not a hindrance, since it shows up the elements with which we must begin our work.

Moreover, it often happens that once the remembered fragments have been interpreted, the patient remembers the rest of the dream and is able to complete the interpretation. The forgotten fragments of the dream are invariably found to represent the most severely repressed elements. By the same token, only after the preliminary interpretation of the remembered fragments is it possible to remember what was forgotten and to interpret what was repressed.

If the patient says he has no dreams, or that he has forgotten them, this conduct must be treated as if it were a neurotic symptom and analyzed in order to understand why the patient reacts in this way. Dreams, like thoughts which are repressed during the day and uncovered at night, often frighten a neurotic patient, and this may be a reason for forgetting. In other cases the reason may be different. One must always discover the meaning of the patient's conduct.

Even without dreams, psychoanalytic treatment may progress normally and without undue delays. It must be clearly understood that the interpretation of dreams is not the only process used by the psychoanalyst to discover a patient's repressions and the genesis of his neurosis. Slips, symptomatic actions, affective transference, daydreams, and, most important of all, the free association of thoughts, are some of the other ways open to the analyst whereby he may deepen his knowledge of the patient's unconscious.

The interpretation of dreams is not always easy. Many dreams may be compared to neurotic symptoms: it is only after long treatment that their psychological meaning can be understood. But in most cases dreams can be interpreted in one or several sessions of psychoanalytic treatment.

The following practical rule is generally followed. If one day the patient relates a dream, the most complete interpretation possible should be attempted; if the dream has not been interpreted, the patient should not be reminded of it the next day, but he should be free to express his thoughts as they come, even though he does not associate them with the dream. The interpretation is pursued only if the patient spontaneously mentions the dream again. This explains why, although it is true that dreams are most easily interpreted during psychoanalytic treatment, it is often necessary to abandon an interpretation. The goal of therapeutic psychoanalysis is, after all, not to analyze dreams but to cure the patient.

Once the analyst has found the interpretation of a dream, he is not always wise to communicate it to the patient; he must always adapt himself to the patient's state of mind. For instance, the first dreams that a patient relates during psychoanalytic treatment are often easily understood through a symbolic interpretation, particularly if the analyst is experienced. The analyst should be restrained not by the fear that his interpretation might be false—it is nearly always confirmed in the course of treatment—but by the fact that the patient's psyche is not yet prepared to confront his repressed thoughts. To avoid psychic traumata the therapist should wait until the patient's efforts bring the repressed unconscious slowly toward consciousness. Metaphorically speaking, it can be said that to communicate an interpretation the analyst must take the last step, carrying the patient with him; all previous steps must be the result of the patient's own efforts.

The analyst must take the last step when the patient is incapable of doing so himself because of intense psychic resistance. Once this resistance is overcome, the analyst often has the impression that his interpretation has opened up a new psychic panorama which was previously inaccessible.

One should not trust interpretations of dreams that the patient makes with extreme ease, nor those that credit the dream with little distortion. These interpretations are generally superficial, if not erroneous, and show that the dream has another, hidden meaning which the patient wishes unconsciously to hide. The analyst himself should follow the same practical rule and mistrust interpretations which he has made too easily.

In some dreams the patient, motivated by transference,

works with a determined unconscious purpose. One type is called a dream of compliance, in which the patient agrees with the analyst. For instance, during recent psychoanalytic sessions the analyst may have interpreted certain acts as homosexual, and some days later the patient has a dream with a manifest homosexual content. Such a dream should be interpreted in relation to the transference. Other dreams, on the contrary, try to deny the analyst's interpretations as well as psychoanalytic assertions. They are known as dreams of opposition.

In order to gauge the correctness of an interpretation, apart from subjective criterion, it is interesting to observe the patient's reaction to what the analyst tells him. Whether the patient agrees or not with the interpretation is only of relative value. An agreement might be a wish to hide the true meaning of the dream, which the analyst has not been able to find; a denial may be an expression of resistance in the face of a correct but unpleasant interpretation. The best objective criterion is the future course of the psychoanalysis and the state of the patient's psyche, since in the course of analysis the problems which first appeared in dreams are often resolved.

A patient's agreement with the analyst's interpretation has a practically certain positive value, if it is accompanied by new memories, such as childhood memories, or some forgotten part of a dream which confirms or completes the given interpretation. The correctness of an interpretation may also be gauged in indirect ways. The patient may make a slip, for instance, or his psychic state may become worse, which indicates that at least one sensitive point of his psyche has been touched.

There are moments in psychoanalysis when the analyst is somewhat confused by the material that the patient has supplied him and that he has not yet understood. What Wilhelm Reich calls a chaotic situation then arises, and possibly every psychoanalytic treatment must go through it. In the midst of this chaotic situation, the interpretation of a dream—which in this case must be as complete as possible, even if it takes several days' work—often supplies a solid and fixed point for arranging the material and continuing the psychoanalytic exploration.

Besides the special conditions of the patient, the analyst's own repressions are the greatest obstacles to the interpretation of dreams. Just as a crystal of a certain color placed before the eye hinders a person from seeing that color in the outside world, the analyst's repressions prevent his seeing the patient's repressions, which, as we now know, constitute one of the sources of dreams. To overcome this obstacle, psychoanalytic institutes in most of the important cities throughout the world require that physicians who wish to become analysts must first submit to a thorough psychoanalysis. Thus, didactic psychoanalysis is the first and most important step in the training of an analyst.

After the didactic analysis, another procedure may be helpful: the auto-interpretation of dreams. In these cases the analyst's dreams should be written down, with all the ideas connected with them, and none should be rejected. As it is often impossible to make the interpretation on the same day, despite every effort, the dream and the written interpretations must be taken up again the following day, and perhaps on a further occasion after more time has elapsed. In this way it may be possible to understand the meaning of one's dreams and help oneself to understand patients' dreams.

One must have great psychic energy and great sincerity to obtain in this way a useful knowledge of one's own unconscious. In most cases this method fails if used instead of formal psychoanalysis; then, people are apt to deceive themselves by saying they are well aware of their own repressions. If any of these people later begin a didactic psychoanalysis, as is often the case, they will find how far they were from discovering their own repressed unconscious through auto-analysis of their own dreams.

Chapter 4

GENITAL SYMBOLISM IN DREAMS

Due to anxiety and ambivalence, and to prohibitions on the part of the super-ego, all of which lead to repression, the genital organs appear with great frequency in dreams. This is illustrated by the following dreams, which have been chosen to facilitate the understanding of dreams by giving examples of very common mechanisms of masking. Most of the dreamers are Argentine, but the symbolism they use is common to everyone.

First we shall examine dreams about *female genital organs.*

10] *In my house; between two armchairs there was a plant which I was watering, and a very beautiful bird came out of it.*

This is the dream of a woman, recently married, who is very happy and wants to have a child. She associated her two breasts *(senos)* with the two armchairs *(sillones)*, the masking made possible through a displacement of similar sounding words.

The plant is her genital organ. This symbolism comes from a day residue—a peach tree that had been planted in her garden. A "peach" is also an ideal woman, according to the commonly used expression; thus her dream means that through marriage she is becoming an ideal and capable woman.

Her husband usually waters the garden and feeds the birds

there. The "watering" in her dream refers to intercourse, and it follows that the beautiful bird which later comes out of the plant is the child she wants. The house at the beginning of her dream is a symbol for her body.

11] *In a round swimming pool. I see other people and among them a woman. The season has not yet begun and the pool is being drained, so that I am in danger in a kind of whirlpool. A woman is also in danger; she must be my fiancée.*

A square swimming pool. There is a child in it. He is told to come out, but he says he still has to soap himself.

I am in a swimming pool, holding on to the edge. A place like a butcher's shop. It has those two doors which open in the middle. The top part has wire netting.

This dream of a man who is worried about his coming marriage is made up of various parts. The last part, the most interesting one in relation to our subject, describes the female genital organ by the two doors, and the wire netting above them represents the pubic hair. It is a butcher's shop because it deals with things of the flesh, and because of the man's destructive fantasies.

Other parts of the dream show his doubts about marriage, a problem which weighs upon him as he has already had sexual relations with his fiancée and would like to establish a home. The patient is in a difficult economic position and is afraid of getting married too soon, this being symbolized by the whirlpool which might swallow him. The draining symbolizes the defloration which has taken place "before the opening of the season," i.e., before marriage.

The other parts of the dream symbolize the man's infantile outlook which impedes his ability to act independently. The square swimming pool is his mother, whom he holds onto as if he were a child. The soaping alludes to masturbation, which he has not made up his mind to stop in order to lead an adult sexual life. Holding onto the edge without going into the water means not daring to lead an independent life by satisfying his desires.

12] *My elder sister brings me a present from my mother. It is one of those conical vases joined directly to the base, but the base is broken, which annoys me. She gives it to me face downwards.*

The vulgar name for the female genital organ in Spanish, French, and English comes from *cunneus,* which means a wedge. Thus the symbolism of the "conic" vase in this dream. The elder sister, who had been idealized by the patient and with whom she partially identified, indicates sexuality which has become devalued by her defloration, represented by the broken base. Being "face downwards" refers to the position preferred by the patient in sexual intercourse.

Generally, any object capable of containing anything may symbolize the female sex, as, for instance, the box in the following dream, which a man dreamed the night after he had definitely broken off intimate relations with a woman. This is expressed by the act of closing:

13] *I close a box.*

An island, or a closed or protected place, can also be a female genital symbol. Such is the case in the following dream of a virgin who does not wish to be so any longer:

14] *A virgin island which is on fire.*

The *hymen* or *defloration* appears frequently in such dreams. Thus the following dream is quite clear:

15] *The mirror of my powder compact had broken.*

This same symbolization of breaking appears in Greuze's painting "The Broken Eggs" [FIGURE 27].

The loss of virginity outside of marriage frequently gives rise to guilt feelings, even in women who do not consciously reproach themselves.

16] *My sister has an all white apron; mine, on the other hand, is torn and dirty.*

In the dream the whiteness represents virginity. The apron worn in front and below the waist symbolizes the female genital organ.

17] *A friend has put on her wedding gown. It is a lace gown. I ask her wonderingly why she has put it on, and she answers that it is not necessary to wait for her wedding day to wear it.*

This is another dream by the same patient, where the symbolism of whiteness is again used. To put on a wedding gown means intercourse, for which the vulgar expression in the Argentine is very similar in sound to the Spanish word for lace. The woman's guilt feelings about her loss of virginity are assuaged in the dream by a displacement onto another woman.

18] *I go to buy fruit with my mother-in-law and another girl. The shop is in front of my house. The door of my house is being enlarged. Moreover, the window seems to be without a frame. There is only a hole; everything can be seen from the street. My younger sister is inside, and I am afraid she will be seen in an untidy state. There is a bookcase covering the entire wall.*

This is another dream by the same woman about the same subject. The mother-in-law represents her future mother-in-law and also her conscience, which reproaches her about her past sexual life. The other girl serves as a point of comparison. To go and buy fruit is to find a male genital organ, in this case her fiancé and marriage. The loss of virginity is an enlarged door and a window without a frame, the double representation being due to the fact that in the past she has had sexual relations with two men. This could cause scandal; in the dream "everything can be seen from the street." All her self-reproaches and criticisms are displaced onto her sister, and the bookcase represents knowledge, partially acquired through books, which she uses to rationalize her past conduct.

In the following dream this same woman solves her problem by making a present of an intact genital organ to another woman, thereby screening her wish of having one herself:

19] *We give Margaret a very small trunk which seems to have a doll inside it.*

The trunk represents the female genital organ. "Small" means intact. The doll represents the hymen and also the child she longs for.

In another dream she symbolizes her conflict by means of shoes:

20] *One of the girls—I think it is my sister—bought shoes like mine. This annoys me and I say I have had these shoes for a long time. In the dream I think they must already be old, and I must change them. I am shown some shoes wrapped in paper as they usually are when sold.*

The shoes are a genital symbol. In many classical paintings virginity is symbolized by a transparent veil covering a woman's belly, and in the dream this appears as the paper around the shoes. The beginning of the dream is an elaboration of guilt feelings due to the woman's loss of virginity, appearing in the dream as annoyance because her sister wants to behave as she does. But the fact that she wants to change her own shoes and get new ones, which means she wishes to cancel her past sexual life, shows her discontent.

The defloration of the women they desire also appears in men's dreams.

21] *A long corridor. The ceiling was all white, except in one place where it was red. I thought that color looked ugly there. There was also a sort of edging that was slightly broken.*

This is the dream of a man who pictures the female genital as a long corridor, and the broken edging means the broken hymen. The red indicates the unpleasant menstruation which is present from time to time; this is symbolized in the dream by putting the color only in one place and not over the entire picture. In other words, a local detail symbolizes something periodic and temporary.

Another man, repelled by the defloration of the woman he loves, has the following dream:

22] A *woman asks me if she is ugly. I answer that she is not, only that she is badly dressed.*

In his associations he compared this woman with another who had a beautiful brooch which she wore on her dress. This jewel represented her virginity.

Similarly, in the next dream, the dreamer rejects the defloration which another man has performed:

23] *I make two women get into a car, first one and then the other.*

I must buy phonograph records in a shop, but I wonder if I shall get there too late, before they close.

In the first part of the dream, the dreamer, annoyed with his fiancée, wishes to avenge himself by behaving as she does—by having previous relations with another woman. But the second part shows his sorrow at knowing that he is too late to be her first man.

The *breasts* may be considered as part of the female genitalia. Two dreams will show some of their symbolizations.

24] *I see a sailing vessel with two beautiful masts painted black. Many smaller boats approach the large one at night to get arms and fuel.*

The ship is a female symbol. Black indicates some physical characteristics of the dreamer's wife. The two masts are her two breasts, and the small boats are the children she has nursed.

25] *Measuring land in Nahuel Huapi. One of the fields had a border of raspberries which had not yet been planted. The land belonged to a woman, and I was going to suggest that she plant some raspberry bushes there.*

In this dream the dreamer wishes to compensate for not having been breast-fed. He associates the fruit (raspberries) with his mother's nipples, which he still desires because of past frustrations. The land is mother earth from whom he wishes to get food; thus it belongs to a woman. The land is Nahuel Huapi, a beautiful spot, indicating the enchantment of oral satisfaction.

Menstruation is often represented in dreams by something alluding to blood or one of its characteristics, such as the color red.

26] *I was giving my husband a bunch of very beautiful red roses which had a lovely smell.*

This is a woman's reaction to her first menstrual period after childbirth. The red flowers symbolize the menstruation which reappears; the lovely smell screens opposite ideas—the woman's fears about the bad odors of her genital organs, caused by guilt feelings about past activity.

Physiologically, menstruation, apart from indicating the non-existence of pregnancy, is the miscarriage of an unfertilized ovum. This is the origin of many dream images of loss and death.

27] *I am going to the doctor's or the dentist's. Blood comes out of my mouth, sometimes clotted. My teeth are loose and they fall out. Two buttons fall off at the same time. I am glad, thinking that now I shall not have to go to the dentist.*

Menstruation is displaced upwards and represented by the bleeding mouth. The falling teeth are the babies who will not be born.

The two buttons derive from a day residue: the eating of a Christmas cake which contained buttons, and the jokes about who would find them—the one who did would remain single and have no children. The buttons are also the two breasts which have lost the joy of nursing since the patient is not pregnant. The doctor or dentist refers to abortions before marriage, because of which the woman feels guilty and physically damaged. Happiness in the dream covers the opposite, sadness.

28] *You were dying. I was weeping desperately. I could feel a tightness in my genitals and then I knew my menstruation had come.*

The appearance of menstruation meant death to the fetus, displaced onto the physician, by whom, due to her transference, the woman wished to have a child. The tears in the dream also symbolize menstruation.

The next day the patient had a toothache, related to the fantasy of the loss of teeth as the loss of children.

The *male genital organ* appears symbolized in many different ways. Thus, in the dream of a recently married woman:

29] *I had had a child. He was not beautiful, but I liked him. My husband's mother was taking me to see the child.*

The details she gave about the child made interpretation easy. "It had a big nose and round eyes. It was already quite big, like a three- or four-month-old baby."

The large nose denotes the penis, and the round eyes, the testicles. That the child was already big indicates an erection. The mother-in-law represents her own mother or her own conscience that permits sexual acts in giving her the child. On another psychological level, the mother is the womb which urges her toward the man.

A girl who had seen her fiancé's genitals for the first time had this dream:

30] *Tiny winged men who wanted to come in through my window.*

For her the dream was a nightmare, because she was sexually afraid and repressed. The tiny men as the penis, the wings as the erection, and the window as the female genital are all clear.

Dreams of this kind allow us to interpret one of Dürer's drawings, "A Dream" [FIGURE 28]. The main figure, the position and placing of which clearly indicate intra-uterine life, is dreaming about an attractive woman. The little angel walking on stilts beside her must mean erection.

The child representing the penis appears in many works of art. Kurt Eissler also points this out, referring to Praxiteles' "Hermes of Olympia" [FIGURE 29]. He holds the child Dionysus in his arms, probably offering him a bunch of grapes. Eissler arrives at this interpretation with the help of a patient's dream: "I am going upstairs and I have a child in my arms," the stairs being the symbol of sexual activity, and the child, the penis. Thus it would symbolize masturbation. On the other hand, in Boardman Robinson's drawing, "The Family" [FIGURE 30], the naked child standing between its parents may symbolize the erect penis in coitus.

31] *An enormously tall cactus bristling with thorns.*

This is the dream of a woman who sees the penis as a cactus. The thorns are the unhappy circumstances of her sexual life, associated with her husband's periodic impotence.

32] *A porter with a big load which almost covers him, and a pistol in the middle of it. X takes the pistol away from me and will not give it back, although I tell him I have returned the 2,000 pesos.*

The load with the pistol is the dreamer's genital organ; he fears castration by X, a brother substitute who caused him anxiety. To overcome his anxiety he submitted to his brother, adopting a passive feminine attitude which appears in the dream as returning the 2,000 pesos. The number 2 represents the femininity he assumed and which he hoped would free him of his castration complex.

33] *I was taking a woman to the hospital so that you could see her, and I was annoyed with you because you would not rise to greet her.*

This is the dream of a homosexual during psychoanalytic treatment. The treatment appears as a hospital, and the woman is the patient himself in his homosexual state. The rising of the psychoanalyst symbolizes erection. In short, the patient is annoyed because the psychoanalyst does not become sexually excited by his presence.

In the two following riddles, the penis is symbolized by one or several of its characteristics, but unlike in dreams, the allusion here is quite transparent and unmistakable. This is so because in the riddles the penis forms only part of the manifest content and nothing of the latent content which is of greater importance. This creates a situation opposite to that of dreams. The latent content being harmless, the unpleasantness produced by a direct manifest allusion can be tolerated by the psyche, and the solution is amusing because it diverts the attention from prohibited subjects.

In ladies' hands
I am nearly always to be found
Sometimes extended,
Sometimes small.
(A *fan*)

It pricks with the point
And pushes with the tail,
And with what hangs
It closes the slit.
(A *needle*)

The serpent is a frequent symbol of the male genital organ, possibly because it is cylindrical in shape and capable of stretching into a shape similar to phallic erection. This symbolism is used in a dream in the following poem.

THE DREAM (from the French *Le Songe*)

Lying with my lover
After the fourth embrace,
I fall asleep at once,
Still lying on my back.
Suddenly I dream
A great serpent is in my hand,
Though flaccid, out erect;
It stretches out
Almost to my foot.

To tell the truth I thought all was lost
When I awoke to find
That what I was holding
Was that which bit Eve.

Another animal which often represents the penis is the fish. This may be observed in Steen's paintings "*La Malade d'Amour*" [FIGURE 31] and "*La Demande Amoureuse Symbolique*" [FIGURE 32]. In the latter the two turnips, as testicles, complete the description of the male genital organ, and the dance shows sexual excitement.

In general, elongated objects are frequently phallic symbols. See, for instance, an easily interpreted cigarette advertisement [FIGURE 33]. The stack in this advertisement also presents symbolizations of the testicles and pubic hair. There is also a repetition of these themes in the symbolism of the uniformed soldier with the large ornate headdress.

Instruments and machines are also frequent male symbols.

34] *A watch with a very prominent winding screw, also the ring around the screw which protects it.*

The dreamer is a person with intense neurotic fears of castration. On the day preceding the dream, one of his relatives stumbled and broke the winding screw of his watch and loosened the case. In the dream this indicates castration, which is compensated in the manifest content. The patient dreams he has a large penis with a large protecting foreskin.

Circumcision is an important source of depressing feelings in man, relating to the castration complex. This appears sometimes in dreams, where either the patient or something belonging to him is not complete. For example:

35] *I see myself without a neck.*

A book with the top part of the paper cover torn, so that the title can be seen.

The title means being a Jew.

36] *With Grace, her sister, and her husband, whom I do not know. They are going to church and invite me to go with them. My trousers are unbuttoned and I cannot go.*

The unbuttoned trousers symbolize the absence of foreskin. Not being able to go to church refers to the social ostracism of the Jew, and, on a deeper and more important level, his psychological inability to allow himself to have sexual intercourse with Grace because of religious differences.

37] *A loaf of bread with the top part cut off.*

The image in the dream suggests circumcision, which was confirmed when the dreamer associated the Spanish word *pan* (bread) with the French word *pain*, and thence to penis. This is a fragment of a long dream connected with the patient's effort in real life to obtain prominent positions in order to compensate for his inferiority complex that he related to his circumcision.

38] *A man had become a minister for the second time. He was telling me that now I could obtain an official position. I was going to the Ministry of the Interior, which was on Diagonal Norte Avenue, and I wished to go to the Casa Rosada* [*where the Ministry of the Interior really is*]. *These buildings were interconnected. Then to a place where there was a loaf of bread with the top part cut off. But this top part was given to me in a drink which tasted very good.*

The details of the dream which have not been interpreted refer to the patient's going back into psychoanalytic treatment in order to become a psychoanalyst. To be appointed minister for the second time means to begin a second analysis.

In his psychoanalysis the patient dwells on the "interior" of his mind, hence the dream image of going to the Ministry of the Interior. But this is only the first step on his way to the Casa Rosada, where the President of the Republic resides; he is, in other words, going to occupy a more prominent position without feeling inferior because of his circumcision.

Circumcision, like some other religious rites, is explained as a hygienic practice. Thus in the final part of the dream the man refers to the drink containing the top part of the loaf, which he "has to swallow," although he does not like it.

This is analogous to the swallowing of a peppermint, with which the following dream of a woman begins. It means having to accept her husband's circumcised penis:

39] *A peppermint. But I swallowed it whole, so I did not taste it.*

I saw a box of little spoons, from which I had to select one. They were coffee spoons. I took one from underneath. When taking it out, I discovered I had made a mistake and had chosen an ice cream spoon. It was wide, but it had a short handle.

The woman who had this dream attributed her discontent to her husband's circumcision. In the second part of the dream, the coffee spoon is a phallic symbol because of its elongated form and the fact that it is put into cups. "It had a short handle" refers to circumcision. To select the spoon from "underneath" is a reminder that she has chosen a husband who is her social inferior. The ice cream spoon indicates her own coldness in intercourse, provoked by her genital devaluation of her husband. After her marriage she found she had "made a mistake"; this is also shown in the dream.

It is easy to find numerous examples of symbolization of *coitus*. They are clearest in the so-called "unwary dreams"—dreams of people who are not in psychoanalytic treatment and mask their hidden desires less ingenuously.

40] *My fiancé from the floor above is pouring water on me, drop by drop. I am on the floor below. I am wearing a strange bathrobe. This happened in a dirty house. I did not know how I happened to be there, but I liked it there.*

The strange bathrobe means that the woman found herself in a strange situation, also that she was undressed. The position of the people and their conduct are without doubt symbols of coitus. The dirty house indicates the woman's low moral evaluation of intercourse, but her liking it there means that she accepts it.

A woman's dream, a year after her husband's death:

41] *Going downstairs on my husband's arm. I could really feel my husband there, feeling the warmth of his flannel suit. It was a wonderful walk.*

In her dream the woman revives her husband and has intercourse with him, symbolized by going downstairs arm in arm with him. The warmth of his flannel suit is an allusion to the warmth of his caresses.

This woman's dream of intercourse is clear:

42] *Wearing a short dress, I dance before some people and gather some fruit.*

The dance and the dress refer to feminine coquettishness and exhibitionism; the fruit symbolizes the male organ she desires. In addition to its unconscious source, the dream also had a conscious source: the woman was to take an examination a few days later; she hoped to pass it successfully and gather the fruits of her labor.

43] *In a shop. I wanted to buy a white cord. A man came and said, "I am taking this cord." Then I was following him, because I wanted him to give me the cord, which I needed. Meanwhile I realized he was the devil. Then a young girl appeared and the man wanted to pursue her. There was a very long staircase, and the man could not reach her because his shoes were falling off. The girl was running and he was running after her, and I wanted to tell the girl that he was not a man but the devil. Then something like an elevator appeared, and I wanted to take it to go up quicker and warn the girl. Then I woke up.*

This is the lightly disguised dream of a naive young woman. The wish to buy something is to desire a man. The cord is the penis. Intercourse is represented by going upstairs and by the pursuit; the dreamer starts the pursuing, but in the course of the excitement she ends by being pursued. Then she makes use of a projection onto another girl to relieve unpleasant moral tensions. The pursuer is converted into the devil as he represents prohibited instincts. (The girl also represents the dreamer's own genital organ.) The shoes falling off indicate a case of impotence, which really occurred once when attempting coitus. During the dream the increasing excitement and the desire to reach orgasm are expressed by the woman's taking the elevator to get upstairs more quickly.

44] *I am surrounded by nymphs dressed in white; a Turk appears with a curved sword.*

This is an easily understandable dream of a thirteen-year-old girl.

In the following dream the cage represents the female genital organ, and the bird the male organ, which is why the cage door is underneath.

45] *A cage with a door underneath and not on the side. The bird was going in and out, and I thought it strange that it did not escape.*

The dreamer woke with an ejaculation after his dream. Birds, or their derivatives—angels—often symbolize the penis in literature, mythology, and art in general, as we can see in Goya's drawing [FIGURE 34]. After intercourse (which is represented in the upper right-hand corner) the prostitutes shoo the "plucked" men out into the street—i.e., plucked both of their money and their potency. The brooms indicate the phallic nature of the women.

Men wanting intercourse appear as birds in one of Penelope's dreams in the *Odyssey* (Canto XIX, lines 509 and following, translated by W. H. D. Rowse):

But please listen to my dream and say what it means. There are twenty great geese about the place which come out of the water to be fed, and it warms my heart to watch them. But a great eagle from the mountains swooped down and broke their necks with his curving claws and killed them. There they lay in a heap on the ground, while the eagle roared up into the sky. I shrieked and cried aloud, I mean in my dream, and a crowd of women gathered about me, as I wept bitterly because the eagle had killed my geese. Back came the eagle again and perched on the free end of a roof beam, and spoke to me with a human voice: "Take courage, thou daughter of far-famed Icarius! This is no dream, but a waking vision of good which will surely be fulfilled. The geese are those who woo thee, and I who was an eagle am now come as thine husband; and I will bring a dreadful death upon them all."

Jupiter as a swan near Leda [FIGURE 35] or as an eagle taking Ganymede to heaven, are also ornithological symbolizations of coitus. Another example of the same theme is found in the drawing "Offensive Amoureuse" [FIGURE 36], in which the birds represent the penis and testicles, and the frog is the woman experiencing pleasure in coitus.

In Shakespeare's sonnet XXIX a man feels miserable (impotent), yearning for what he does not possess. But the image of the woman he loves appears.

> Yet in these thoughts myself almost despising
> Haply I think on thee: and then my state,
> Like to the lark at the break of day arising
> From sullen earth, sings hymns at Heaven's gate . . .

The lark in flight is the phallic erection; heaven represents the vagina, and the singing of hymns symbolizes coitus.

In Viladrich's painting "The Dream of a Young Boy" [FIGURE 37], a man is represented by a bird. It is the powerful oedipal father against whom the son fights with his knife, the shape and position of which indicate phallic symbolism. The submission of son to father is duplicated by the sheep near the claws of the vulture. In the rock that shelters the young boy, one can surmise a woman's silhouette, clearly apparent in the tracing [FIGURE 38]. This refers to the mother who shelters the son in her womb and whose love strengthens him and motivates the oedipal conflict.

All these elements are unintentionally represented by the painter and without his conscious awareness, guided by his profound intuitive artistic inspiration.

46] *A narrow gate in the country which was swinging back and forth. I was on horseback, and when the horse saw the gate it became restless and stood on its hind legs. I continued riding.*

The symbols in this dream are the gate as the female genital and the rampant horse as the penis in erection. The swinging gate represents sexual excitement and coitus. The dreamer was a woman, and from the characteristics of her dream it can be deduced that she was somewhat virile.

Riding on horseback is a frequent symbol of coitus. As a literary illustration let us quote García Lorca's poem, "The Unfaithful Bride," from the "Romancero Gitano," in which a man describes the gratification of his desire for a woman in the following way:

Aquella noche corrí	That night I had
El mejor de los caminos	The best ride of my life,
Montado en un potro de nacar	Mounted on a pearly mare
Sin bridas y sin estribos.	Without bridle or stirrups.

47] *I went on board ship with my wife. I was in evening dress. I remember perfectly I was wearing a stiff shirt. My parents were bidding me goodbye. I think they were dressed as I was.*

This is the dream of a man whose strained marital relations caused a temporary sexual rift with his wife. Because of his unsatisfied instinctual desires he dreams of the beginning of his sexual life with his beloved wife during their honeymoon. The evening dress symbolizes being naked and sexually excited. The stiff shirt is the penis in erection, displaced upwards. To go on board ship is to have intercourse, and he obtains his parents' moral consent as they bid him farewell. Their sexual life is an example for him, for they are dressed as he is in the dream.

48] *I was trying to sell a length of cloth to my wife. I think I had three lengths, and I wanted to sell her the middle one, telling her it was the prettiest.*

This was dreamed by the same person as the previous dream, and the motive was the same. Three is a male genital symbol, the middle one of the three lengths being quite clear in meaning.

49] *Some Hindus take me to a pit which is covered by three bars on which they place me. They heat these bars, or make an electric current go through them, to the point where I cannot bear the heat and must drop into the pit which is full of lions and tigers. I feel a certain sense of pleasure when I have to do this.*

Here intercourse is indicated in a masochistic way because of the dreamer's fears. The Hindus are strange as are his sexual instincts, which urge him toward women whose sex appears as a pit. The three bars are the penis, which is anatomically formed by the two *corpora cavernosa,* and by the *corpus spongiosum*—as the dreamer, who was a doctor, knew. The increasing electric current is the growing excitement which leads to ejaculation, as represented by his falling into the pit. The lions and tigers symbolize all his fears about the vagina, based on painful experiences of venereal diseases. But in spite of everything, he does not fail to experience pleasure in the end.

50] *I am riding in a car with other people, but I do not think it wrong because Frank and Anthony are also doing it.*

A day residue of the dream was the strike of the town's bus drivers. As an emergency measure taxis were allowed to carry separate passengers together. This obliged the girl to ride with unknown people, under municipal orders—unconsciously an authorization to "go with others," to have coitus (co-ire: to go together). The sense of guilt is also silenced in the dream by the presence of two other people who had had illicit relations with women. The fact that there were several people in the car gratifies the dreamer's polygamous tendencies.

51] *With my cousin in the subway. My cousin was with his daughter.*

As in the former dream, traveling with someone represents coitus. The daughter, besides symbolizing her genital organ, indicates the incestuous quality which the dreamer invests in her sexual attraction to her cousin.

To walk along a road also symbolizes coitus. Thus, according to legend, Oedipus met and killed his father while driving his chariot along a road. The road had deep crevices, or, in another version, an intersection where three roads met. The symbolism of the vagina in the first road is easy to understand, but the symbol of the intersection is more obscure. Karl Abraham is able to interpret it through a patient's dream in which "the desecrated tomb of his mother was in a place where two streets met a main thoroughfare." The latent meaning was that of coitus with the mother, the streets representing the two legs and the torso which are joined together at the point where the genital organs are situated. In this way we understand that the conflict of the intersection in the Oedipus legend describes his fight with his father to obtain his mother's genital organ.

52] *On the doorstep of your house, with my two sisters. I think it is time for my psychoanalytic session, but I do not go up yet. Your wife comes and asks if you have arrived, calling you by your first name, Angel. I see you coming. You are wearing one of those hats that usually have a tiny feather. But you have an enormous feather which makes me laugh. In the hall there is a bench, and I go in to continue laughing.*

This woman is dreaming of intercourse. Beyond the rejecting words in the manifest content one can easily guess the mounting excitement and final acceptance. All this is part of her affective transference to the psychoanalyst.

The doorstep represents the dreamer's genital organ. It is part of the analyst's house to show her instinctual leaning toward him, as if she were confessing she belonged to him. The two sisters symbolize her breasts.

The analyst's wife appears as an obstacle which forces her to greater repression; but in the dream the wife also represents the dreamer, imagining marriage with the analyst, for she calls him by his first name, which is quite unlike her usual conduct. The hat is the penis, and the erection is indicated by the size of the feather. The dreamer's defense against these sexual contents is expressed by her attempt to ridicule the situation. Finally, the bench represents the bed toward which she goes, always hiding her surrender behind her laughter.

This conduct in the dream had its counterpart in real life, before psychoanalytic treatment began. The first time the woman had intercourse with her husband, she was unable to overcome a persistent and involuntary giggle.

A woman dominated by sexual desires which she considers wicked finds it impossible to refuse coitus, and this appears in the following dream:

53] *I am in a concentration camp. There are many officers walking in a circle. In front of each man there is a woman in evening dress. I find it difficult to walk because my dress is very long. I have the impression that I am a prostitute. Outside the camp I see a man with an enormous butcher knife in his hand. He is kneeling by a corpse that I cannot distinguish clearly. The man sticks the knife deeply into the flesh. He takes it out and stabs again and again and again. . . . I awaken horrified.*

Penis et cultelus non sunt idem, exclaims a confessor in a popular old story, when he finds that women confess prohibited intercourse by saying merely that "they sheathed the dagger." The day residue for this dream was a conversation about the raping of a woman in a concentration camp. In the dream, intercourse is shown as a sadistic and necrophilic act; the dreamer avoids anxiety by means of a projection. She "cannot distinguish clearly" because she herself is the corpse. Evening dress indicates sexual excitement, and the officers walking in a circle is a projection onto men of the way prostitutes walk around.

The wish to prostitute herself is even clearer in the following dream, dreamed by a woman in financial difficulties.

54] *I enter a shop to buy something. I speak to a salesgirl, but instead of asking her to show me what I wish to buy, I tell her I am looking for work. The salesgirl answers that she must see the boss for that. She returns and says, "If you wish, you can come every day from five to seven. The boss says that it is pleasant work and that he will pay 50 pesos a day."*

It is not only in dreams that prostitution appears disguised. Thus in a cartoon [FIGURE 39] coitus is represented by the word "exchange" in reference to a bank. The bank appears because the girl is a prostitute, guided by monetary motives rather than love. The female genital organ is symbolized by the "night deposit vault," and the male organ by the column. The comic effect is produced by means of easily understandable symbols and the ingenuity with which they are expressed.

55] *I had a child on my lap and was taking care of it. The child was vomiting.*

This is a dream of *masturbation.* The child is the penis. To care for it symbolizes masturbation, and vomiting indicates ejaculation.

Something akin to vomiting, and also symbolizing masturbation, may be seen in the following dream.

56] *I had something white in my throat that I wanted to get rid of by moving my entire body. In the end I had to use my hand to bring it out.*

The white stuff is semen; the throat is the penis. At first the dreamer fights against masturbation, but in the end he decides to accept it.

57] *I knock up against an automobile and my head bleeds.*

The automobile (self-movement), according to the patient's associations, represents masturbation in this dream. Blood is substituted for semen.

Because masturbation is effected with the fingers, it is sometimes symbolized by the number five or by playing the piano, as in the next dream of a woman who disguises an occasion when she masturbated a man.

58] *A friend of mine comes, wakes me up, and begs me to play a piece by Ravel. I get up and begin to play, but when I finish the piece I am ashamed of myself because I made five mistakes.*

The mistakes in the dream allude to the five fingers of her hand masturbating the man. One finger more, i.e., six on each hand, shows female masturbation in Picasso's "A Dream" [FIGURE 40]. Possibly the fact that it is a supplementary and abnormal finger indicates sexual activities with these characteristics. This interpretation was obtained by asking people who were being analyzed for their associations to that detail of the picture. Since many answers coincided, there was some validity about the interpretation. The same method was used to interpret other details: thus the appearance of the face suggested fellatio; the black part covering the lower region, the pubic hair; and the necklace suggested excitation of the breast. Thus the whole picture is made up of various sexual activities which are autoerotically satisfied as part of the sleeping woman's dream. By applying our knowledge of symbolism it was possible to make further interpretations, but with a little more reserve. The three vertical lines represent man and the male sex; woman would be represented by the two lines, which in contact with the first three represent intercourse. Finally, the rhomboids and flowers might be seen as female bellies with fetal contents.

59] *A sister of mercy shakes hands with me.*

This is also a dream of masturbation, symbolized by shaking hands. It refers to the dreamer's childhood masturbation with his sister. In the manifest content she appears as a sister "of mercy," because of the relief she produced by diminishing his instinctual tensions—which he would like to see revived in another present-day situation.

60] *Louise and I were spreading marmalade on bread.*

The bread stands for the penis (in Spanish, *pan* means bread, *pene* means penis), and to spread something sweet on it means pleasant masturbation. The dreamer was in love with Louise.

In Spanish-speaking countries *paja* (straw) is a common name for masturbation, so that it appears symbolized in that form in dreams.

61] *There was a fire somewhere, and I was annoyed because it had started through carelessness. The end of the couch was burning, and I was surrounded by flames. People escaped from the other side, and I thought they were wrong because the floor was made of straw and they would fall through. Then I ran through the fire and was saved. I was already safe. In any case, I would not have dropped down like the others through the straw, because I would have chosen to be asphyxiated by gas. The other way would have been a miserable death. I chose either to be saved or to be asphyxiated.*

The symbolism is clear: the dreamer was a woman patient fighting against a violent love for her psychoanalyst. She wishes to be free of the desire but decides that to do so she must not return to her previous neurotic reserve, when she masturbated (death and the straw floor). Instead she must face the transference boldly and dare to assert her sexual desires. The couch is the analyst's, and the fire symbolizes her love. The asphyxiation refers to her wish for, at least, kisses on the mouth.

The following dreams are of married men fighting against the desire to masturbate, which has various causes.

62] *I say to myself that the fight against communism must start. With G.D., I am slapping and hugging her. I do not know if I have had an ejaculation.*

G. D. is an actress. In the dream she represents the penis, which is commonly given feminine names, and thus appears as a woman. Slapping her is masturbation, confirmed by the ejaculation in the manifest content.

The first part alludes to the dreamer's wife; he is discontented with her and it starts him thinking of autoerotic activity. On one occasion his wife defended communism; to fight against communism is therefore to attack her. On a deeper level, communism means life "in common" with the wife he no longer loves and whom he would like to leave, going back to masturbation.

Masturbation sometimes awakens in the child a fear of castration by his parents. This is what is hidden in the dreams of a four-year-old child, told to us literally by his mother:

63] *I dreamed you took away my lampshade and gave me Louise's. I did not want it because hers had a hole in the middle.*

I dreamed that instead of the lampshade I had a rope. Mario and I were together, and we took turns pulling the rope up and down.

Pulling the rope describes the child's masturbation with a friend. Taking away the lampshade means castration as a punishment. There is, then, a substitution of his male genitals for those of a girl friend whom he considered castrated.

Impotence in men and frigidity in women are among the most painful sexual disturbances. The following dreams deal with *impotence*.

64] *I was walking and my legs seemed to become paralyzed, and I could not go any further.*

In this case the impotence of the male organ is represented as paralysis of the legs. Coitus is symbolized by walking.

The symbolization is different in other cases:

65] *I am in a room with my brother; we are both lying down. Someone comes in and my brother tells me, but I cannot get up.*

The brother symbolizes the penis. The lack of erection is observed in the dreamer's failure to rise when someone enters the room, i.e., when he is with a woman, someone he comes into contact with.

Don Quixote's dream in the Cave of Montesinos is clearly a dream of impotence. It is in two parts. In the first, the ghost of a knight, Durandarte, appears and continually begs one of his relatives to wrench the heart from his breast and give it to his beloved Belerma. But later we find that this relative had already faithfully fulfilled the request, as shown by the fact that Belerma, an old and ugly woman, appears carrying Durandarte's heart in her hand.

The second part of the dream becomes more personal. Dulcinea appears and asks Don Quixote for a small amount of money, offering her petticoat as security. Richer in imagination than in money, Don Quixote gives her a smaller amount and refuses the petticoat.

The knight Durandarte in the first part represents Don Quixote himself, aged fifty, who, obeying the mandate of his super-ego and the deficiencies of his age, rejects his love for a socially inferior peasant girl of loose morals. The rejection is represented in the dream by the opposite, since the beloved Belerma holds the gentleman's dried heart in her hand. But the rejection of the sexual desire is shown by the fact that Durandarte is a ghost, and by the presence of the relative whom the knight reproaches constantly for not having delivered his heart to the lady.

In the second part of the dream the latent content is easier to perceive. The lack of money symbolizes deficient potency, and the petticoat, which Dulcinea offers him, is her genital organ, which Don Quixote cannot accept.

Psychosis diminishes Don Quixote's mental tensions, since his sensual love is converted into easy platonic love. In this he obeys his super-ego, which also directs his chivalrous adventures. Because they are ridiculous and masochistic, they show mockery of his super-ego.

66] *My husband and I are going to a gala evening. My mother-in-law, who knows I do not have an evening gown, lends me hers, a beautiful white one. My husband has no problems. He has his tails and starched shirt. While we are dressing, I find that the maid has washed the shirts but they are not starched. I show one to my husband, hoping it will do, but it is no good. Then I show him another, and that is no good either. The same thing happens with a third one. My husband says, "I've had it." Everybody goes to the party and we stay at home.*

The stiff shirt is the penis in erection. Its not being starched symbolizes the husband's impotence, which had occurred some days before. The patient blames herself for this situation because of her lack of genital excitability, which appears in the dream as if the maid—the dreamer—had not starched the shirt. (Actually the woman's rejection of genitality contributed to the husband's impotence.) The dreamer's lack of confidence in her own instinctual capacity also appears in the dream as her lacking an evening gown; it must be borrowed from her mother-in-law, whom she considers to have a model sexual life.

In the dream there are three shirts because the wife thought that men had three testicles; also, because frequently three is a male symbol. Not being able to go to the party means rejecting coitus, which others are able to accomplish.

In general, everything which is not capable of standing up may symbolize impotence—for example, the unstarched shirt in the previous dream, and the man and branch in FIGURE 42, which is an advertisement for a medical aphrodisiac. On the other hand, the cock with its head held high represents genital erection. The characteristics of the cock, with his protruding gland, also allude to masculine morphology.

FIGURE 1. Goya: Nightmare

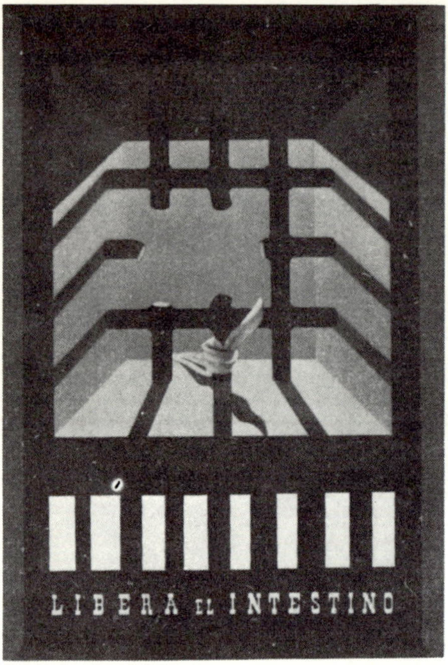

FIGURE 2. A Prisoner Has Escaped

FIGURE 3. A Clean Sweep

FIGURE 4. Circulation

FIGURE 5. The Critical Age

FIGURE 6. Making Use of the Current

FIGURE 7. Natural Rhythm

FIGURE 8. Rain (in French, gonorrhea is called "the military drop")

FIGURE 9. Rhinitis

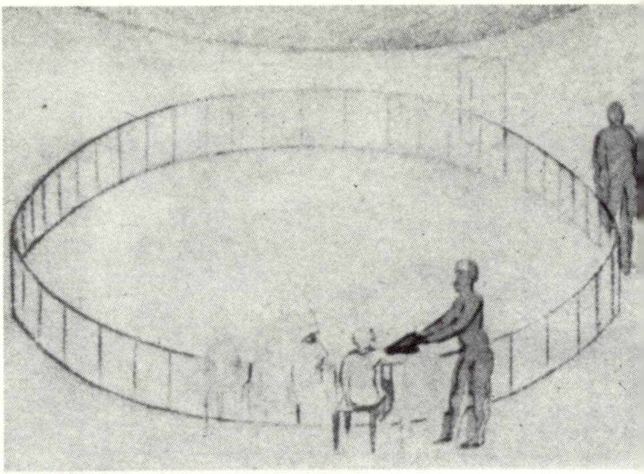

FIGURE 10. A Narrow, Oval Room

FIGURE 11. "I Go on Board" (1)

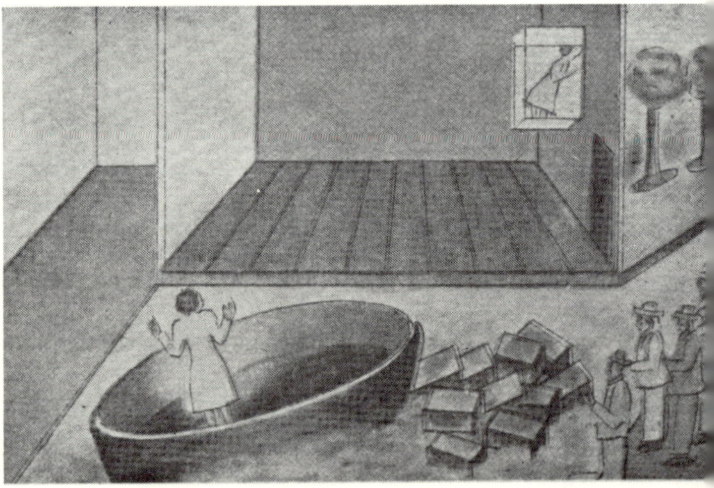

FIGURE 12. "I Go on Board" (2)

FIGURE 13. The Red Cap

FIGURE 14. The Bird of Paradise

FIGURE 15. Red and Yellow

FIGURE 16. The Madman Who Was Fishing

FIGURE 17. Display of Lights

FIGURE 18. Lino Palacio: The March Past

FIGURE 19. Goya: The Dream of Lies and Inconstancy

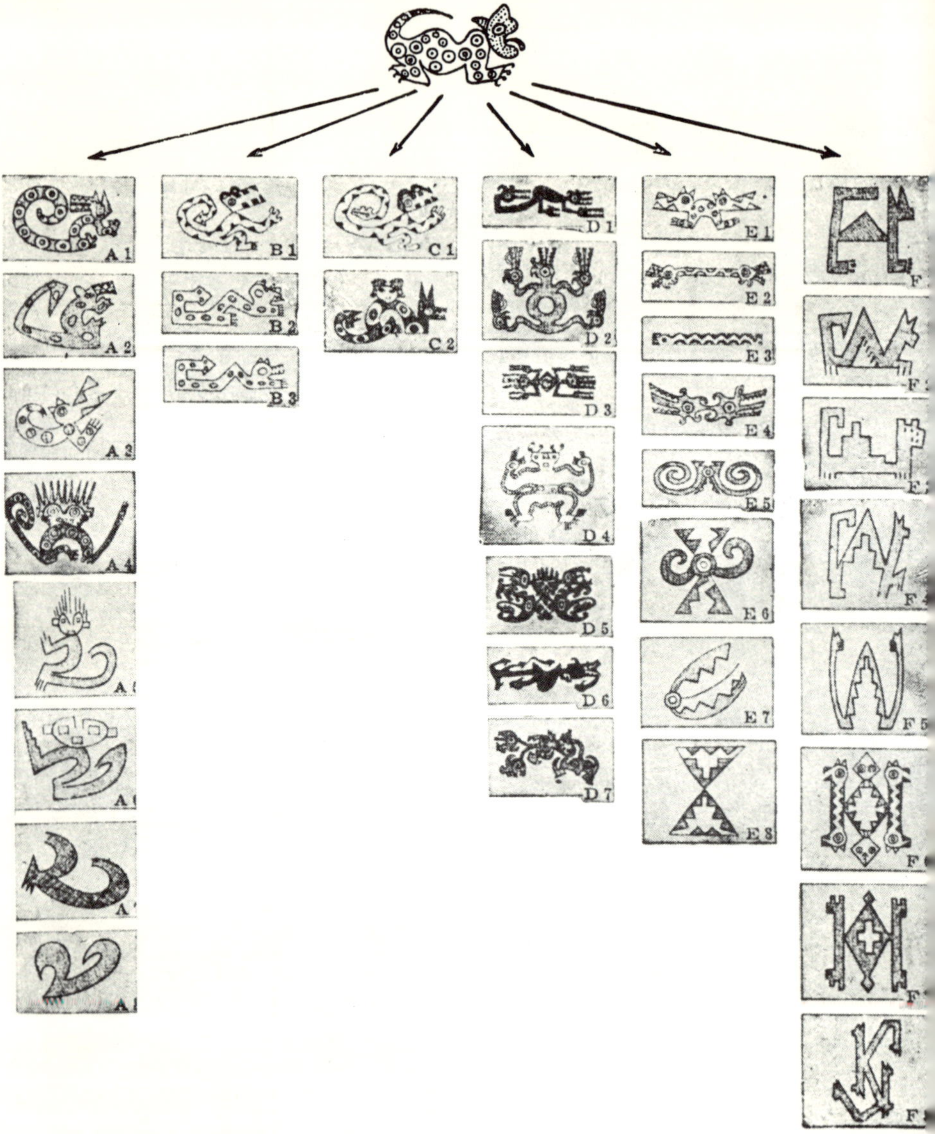

FIGURE 20. Antonio Serrano: The Feline Motive of the Diaguita Indians

FIGURE 21. Duo (1)

FIGURE 22. Louis Boilly: Nina's Prelude

FIGURE 23. Duo (2)

FIGURE 24. Duo (3)

FIGURE 25. "Stop Playing with that Damned Violin and Let's Do Things Properly"

FIGURE 26. Duo (4)

FIGURE 27. Greuze: The Broken Eggs

FIGURE 28. Dürer: A Dream

FIGURE 29. Praxiteles: Hermes of Olympia

FIGURE 30. Boardman Robinson: Family

FIGURE 31. Steen: Lovesick

FIGURE 32. Steen: A Symbolic Proposal of Love

FIGURE 33. Cigarettes

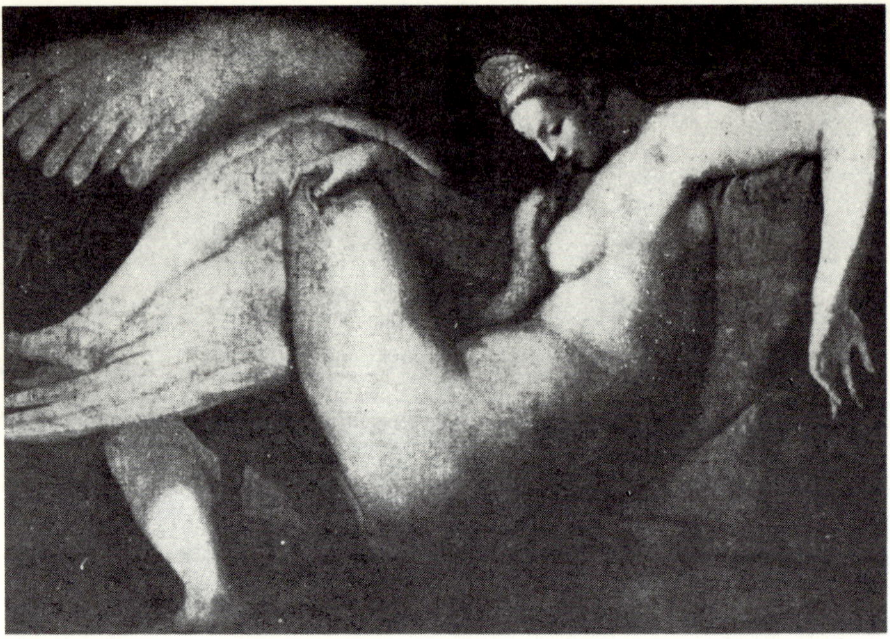

FIGURE 35. Michelangelo: Leda

FIGURE 34. Goya: They Have Already Been Plucked

FIGURE 36. Amorous Offensive

FIGURE 37. M. Viladrich: The Boy's Dream

FIGURE 38. A Tracing of "The Boy's Dream" (FIGURE 37)

FIGURE 39. Cobean: The Bank

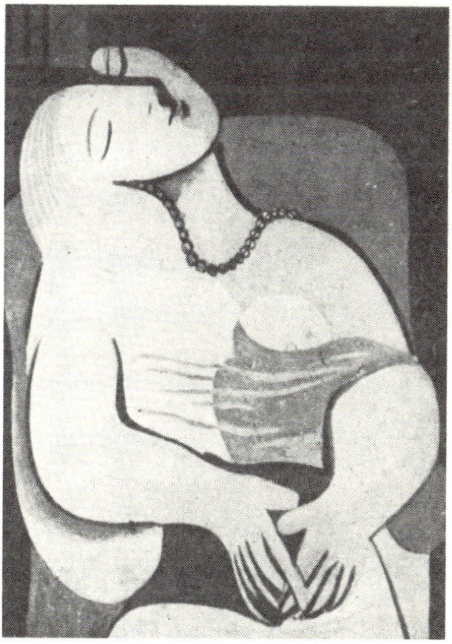

FIGURE 40. Picasso: A Dream

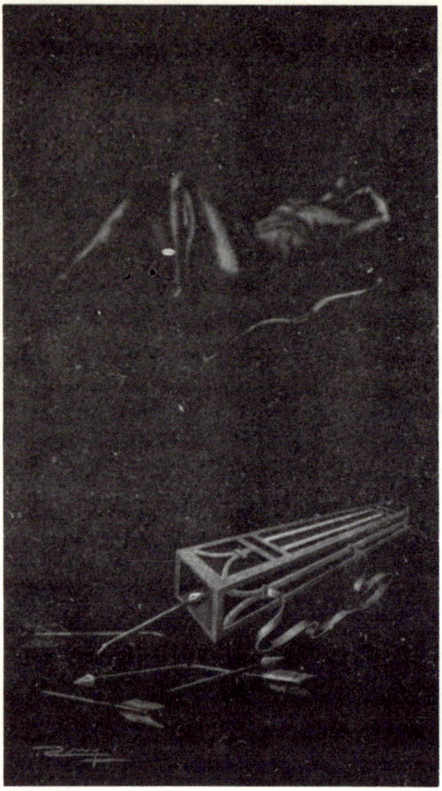

FIGURE 41. The Archer

FIGURE 42. Depression

FIGURE 43. William Blake: Queen Kathleen's Dream

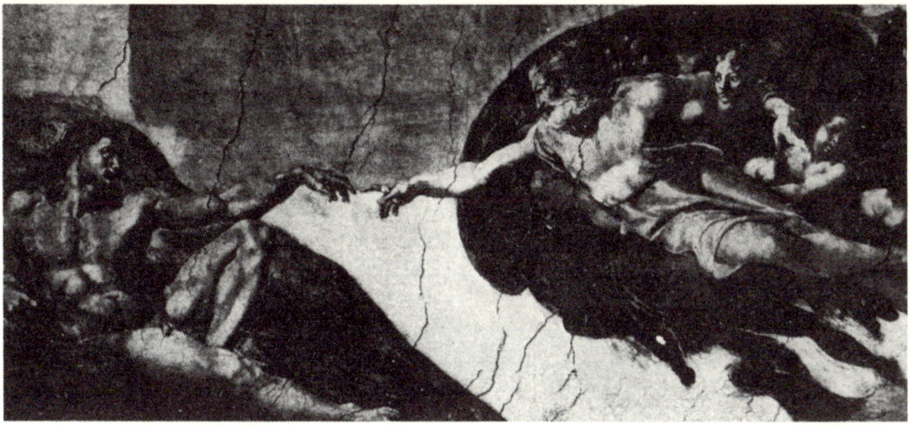

FIGURE 44. Michelangelo: The Birth of Man

FIGURE 46. Boticelli: The Birth of Venus

FIGURE 47. The Dream of King Babar

As we have seen in the last case, in the psychoanalytic treatment of male impotence we must consider the characteristics both of the patient and his sexual partner. Improvement in the woman often acts favorably upon the man, in cases where his inhibitions stem mainly from her. In other instances, improvement in one partner may disrupt a stable, if unhappy, equilibrium.

67] *My toothbrush is broken. I can see the top part has come off. It is in the bathroom cabinet; I try to repair it by placing it on the highest shelf of the cabinet.*

In this dream of impotence, the unconscious idea of the castrated penis appears as a toothbrush with the top part broken off. The bathroom cabinet represents the dreamer's attempt to cure himself, since he associates the cabinet with a place where medicines are kept. The top shelf means the mouth, indicating the dreamer's fancy of fellatio for sexual gratification, since coitus is impossible due to his impotence.

Dreams of ejaculatory impotence are less frequent than those of erectile impotence. Here is an example of the former:

68] *I dreamed about a German general who killed three hundred Italian patriots in the Adriatine caverns.*

This was a physician's dream, following intercourse without ejaculation. The cruel general is himself, for he destroyed the spermatozoa in the *corpora cavernosa* of the penis, when he "ardently" desired coitus, instead of letting them fulfill their "patriotic" function, which meant paternity. There are three hundred because three symbolizes phallic potency.

Male impotence, or fear of it, causes a reaction in women.

69] *I am in a room with President Roosevelt. I know I must help him to cross the room, ahead and to the right. I realize that he is an important person, but I am not afraid. When I help him to rise, I am surprised to find how easy it is. It is not necessary to make any effort, and I am happy. He has his arm around me, but I do not perceive I am helping him.*

The dreamer was a woman who had lived in the United States.

For various reasons she feared the impotence of the man she loved and with whom she had not yet had sexual relations. President Roosevelt, with his paralysis, represents the man's penis. To rise is erection, and to cross the room, coitus. In the dream the woman happily attains a satisfactory sexual relationship with normal potency.

Frigidity may be symbolized in various ways:

70] *You came to my house. There was a large table. But the things to be given to you had either not been brought to me or else I could not find them.*

The woman relives her genital frigidity in the dream, with the analyst as her object, through the displacement to other people. She wants to surrender sexually but cannot do so, representing this by "things" she wants to give but cannot find. The large table is the bed, where she wants to satisfy her apparently great desires. The size of the table is a reversal of a childhood situation in which she suffered hunger—a small table—this being one of the sources of her renunciation of instinctual satisfactions.

Sexual surrender symbolized by giving food is seen in the following dream:

71] *Lots of people in my house, and I am worried because there is nothing to offer them. The maid has not prepared anything, although the food is there. I am quickly preparing something, but there is no time. There is also a large jug of wine, but I am annoyed because the maid has broken off a piece of it. My older sister comes and tells me not to hurry because there is something good in the Frigidaire: pineapple and ham. I agree with her but tell her there is not enough.*

The servant is herself or her genital organs, or perhaps also her husband who does not excite her before intercourse. Lots of people in her home represent her husband expressing great sexual excitement toward her and having intercourse. The wish to give them something is her desire to respond with a satisfactory orgasm.

"No time" refers to her inability to reach orgasm at the same time as her husband, while the broken jug is her deflorated vagina, for which she harbors resentment against her husband, following unconscious thoughts (similar to those which Freud has shown in "The Taboo of Virginity"). It is also hatred toward her husband for exciting her sexually.

With the help of her older sister, one of her models for sexual life, things improve and she is less frigid, symbolized by taking the pineapple and ham out of the Frigidaire. The pineapple and ham also allude to her mother and a thrilling party which she attended with her husband.

72] *I had been promised candy for a party I had to give. Some days before, I call to make sure I will receive it, and I am told they will be unable to send it. I am most indignant and feel very bad about it.*

Here also food symbolizes genital satisfaction, the candy being the sweetness of sexual orgasm which the woman cannot attain. Her indignation is directed toward the psychoanalyst, to whom she came because of her frigidity and who cannot promise an immediate cure.

73] *I am combing my hair to go on an excursion to X. But I cannot curl my hair properly. Looking out through the window, I see it is raining, and I think it is just as well for then I do not need to go.*

Going somewhere symbolizes coitus, and the rain, ejaculation. The window is the vagina where the woman feels the genital discharge of the husband. Her inability to reach orgasm is symbolized by her inability to curl her hair. She consoles herself by accepting the situation, giving up the trip to X—a pleasant place, but one where the owners forbid the gathering of flowers or fruit. The owners represent her parents who prohibited sexual satisfaction and obliged their daughter to be frigid.

74] *My husband and I were going to the movies with my brothers-in-law and their wives. Later they wanted to go* *dancing. We could not go because of our daughter. I went home sadly. Later my sister-in-law telephoned to say that they had not gone either.*

The woman hopes for, but fails to attain, total sexual satisfaction, which she thinks the others around her, represented by her brothers-in-law and their wives, are achieving. The movies represent her sexual fantasies and preliminaries to coitus. To go dancing is coitus and orgasm. She cannot go because of her daughter—her genital organs, which are not sufficiently excitable. She consoles herself thinking that many others are in the same position.

75] *I fall and this produces anxiety.*

76] *I want to get somewhere and I cannot.*

77] *I want to shoot, but the bullet fails to come out.*

These are all dreams of impotence by a woman who is anxious about intercourse, which is represented in her dreams by a fall.

78] *You come to my house. I am preparing a cup of tea for you, but when I bring it to you, you have already left.*

I am dressing quickly because some visitors have arrived. I hurry and in my dream I have an orgasm.

In the first dream the man has a genital discharge before the dreamer does. The house symbolizes the vagina. But in the second dream she reaches orgasm, represented by being able to dress quickly, indicating excitement. In the first dream she brings the cup of tea, which may be her vaginal lubrication, too slowly.

Dressing as a symbol of sexual excitement appears in another dream:

79] *I must meet Peter and I cannot find any clothes to wear. Then they bring me the roses I ordered. But instead of being pretty roses, they are ugly, small, and faded.*

The woman does not reach the necessary level of sexual excitement—clothes—so the pleasure she gets from intercourse is insignificant, represented by the small roses.

80] *I am with my wife sleeping in a room which is not mine. I am cold but I have no blanket to cover myself with.*

This man is married to a frigid woman. He feels attracted to her and has intercourse, represented in the dream by sleeping, but he fails to obtain the warmth he seeks. His wife is incapable of giving warmth. The husband would like to be in different circumstances since he has normal sexual reactions. Thus the room in the dream means that the reactions he must have toward his wife do not satisfy him.

Pregnancy may appear in dreams under the guise of getting wet or soiled by something.

81] *I was under the shower and suddenly I discovered I had forgotten to put on my rubber cap. I told myself it was two days since I had washed my hair and it was a bother to have to dry it again. I repeated that it was a bother, and I could see the water falling and wetting my hair.*

This woman is protesting against a possible pregnancy after twice having intercourse—"two days"—without precautions (not wearing a rubber cap, which symbolizes her contraceptive device). The fertilization is symbolized by getting wet, and her displeasure is evident in the dream.

82] *I was going up in an elevator with my husband. There was a notice reading "wet paint," so we avoided leaning against the sides, but my husband playfully pushed me against the side. I got angry because I stained my dress.*

To go up in the elevator with her husband means coitus, and the notice reading "wet paint" is a warning against pregnancy, the paint representing the fertilizing semen. The husband does not take the necessary precautions, and so she gets her dress (uterus) dirty, i.e., pregnant.

Another dream by the same woman was brought on by an identical situation.

83] *I am walking down the street with my daughter. I meet my mother, who cannot control herself when she sees my daughter. She takes her into her arms and kisses her, although this displeases me.*

The mother represents the womb (matrix) harboring a new child, this being symbolized by lifting and kissing the first child. To walk along the street is coitus, and the child also symbolizes the patient's genital organ.

In William Blake's painting "Queen Kathleen's Dream" [FIGURE 43], the flying figures must represent children. This interpretation seems to be confirmed by the fact that the whole group bears a certain resemblance to the anatomic appearance of the uterus and vagina. We find the same thing in Michelangelo's "The Birth of Man" [FIGURE 44], where the mantle is the pregnant womb and belly, and the nine children within it are the fetus, indicating by their number the nine months of pregnancy.

84] *Balloons that rise and burst. Two cats jump out of one of them. I offer my wife one of them.*

Pregnancy is represented by the belly—balloons—which by increasing in size brings forth children—cats—which the man's wife longs for. In the same way pregnancy appears as a balloon in Steig's cartoon "The Pregnant Woman" [FIGURE 45].

Childbirth is symbolized by a fall or drop from somewhere; thus the French *mettre bas* and the German *niederkommen*. It is also symbolized by a relationship to water, which is frequent in mythological and folkloric narratives. An example of this is Botticelli's well-known "The Birth of Venus" [FIGURE 46], where the goddess comes out of a shell surrounded by water. Winds may allude to the sensation of cold a newborn baby must feel when it comes into contact with the outside air.

FIGURE 45. Steig: A Pregnant Woman

Dreams of pregnancy may appear during psychoanalytic treatment, when the patient decides to pass from one psychological situation to another. For example, when he wants to abandon a passive homosexual position and behave actively. The radical change of situation is expressed by indicating a former radical change, from the mother's womb to the outside world.

Chapter 5

GENITAL CONFLICTS

During psychoanalytic treatment we can see clearly the process of the dream work by the study of a series of dreams of one person. We may observe in them the different symbolizations and other types of disguise under which the same latent content appears in the manifest content of the dreams. Moreover, as the patient is gradually freed from repressions in the course of treatment, the hidden elements became more and more recognizable.

We can see this process in the following dreams of a woman in her forties who longed for adequate sexual gratification but who was also very inhibited. In her first dreams the symbolism is obscure, but after several months of treatment the ego accepts what was formerly repressed.

85] *I am wrapped in bandages as if I had had an operation.*

Interpretation through associations showed that on a superficial level the dream represented the patient's sexual inhibitions in the form of the bandages that held her and prevented her freedom of movement. Deeper associations showed that the operation had the meaning of an instinctual liberation. In fact, the patient associated this element of the dream with various operations her women friends had undergone. These were women whose sexual life could hardly be considered normal, and this, according to the patient, caused libidinal accumulation and a number of organic troubles that had to be treated surgically. From this it was possible to deduce that the operation in the dream for her held the meaning of a sadomasochistic sexual act, in which the surgeon's knife and the wound symbolized the male and female organs.

Another of her dreams had manifest and latent contents analogous to the previous one:

86] *A friend of mine, all wrapped in bandages as if she were badly wounded, goes to the place where she works to ask for a few days leave of absence until she is cured.*

A *bunch of turnips or carrots.*

The friend is someone with whom the patient identifies, since she also has inadequate libidinal gratification and a number of neurotic symptoms. These symptoms are represented by her being "all wrapped up in bandages as if she were badly wounded." To ask for a leave of absence in order to be cured is to ask for an authorization to seek sexual gratification which would alleviate her troubles; and the person who is asked for the leave of absence, and who does not appear in the dream, symbolizes the patient's conscience, or its infantile source, the parents.

The second part of the dream represents the desired genital object in the shape of a clearly phallic symbol.

87] *My younger daughter had white lice on her head, but below the hairline, on the nape of her neck. They looked like peach stones. I thought that, of course, now that spring was coming . . .*

The lice of this dream stand for genital sensations. Although at first this may seem odd, they have this meaning because lice are insects which move over the skin producing cutaneous excitation akin to the genital excitation of the skin.

Moreover, the patient suffers from leucorrhea, which in her, as in other women, is associated with sexual dissatisfaction. She associates the leucorrhea with the white color of the lice. "Younger daughter" frequently symbolizes the female genitalia.

The other element, "below the hairline, on the nape of the neck," indicates the pubic hair and the upper part of the vagina, where genital excitation is felt most intensely. Finally, the arrival of spring further confirms the interpretation that the dream is provoked by unsatisfied genital excitation.

Only the peach stones could not be fully interpreted, but possibly they allude to the male sex glands, which were frequently the object of her fantasies during genital excitation. This fantasy produced in her a genital excitation with sensations (lice) in the vagina (on the nape of her neck), and also leucorrhea (white lice) due to the lack of libidinal gratification.

88] *My hands were white and swollen, and no one came to help me and save me from death.*

This dream is easy to interpret when we know one of the patient's associations. According to her, she had her hands on her chest while she was dreaming. From this we can deduce that what appears in the manifest content as white, swollen hands, represents in the latent content her breasts full of unsatisfied libido and the desire to be caressed by hands. Bearing in mind this unpleasant content, we need not go far to find the latent meaning of her cry for help, i.e., intercourse.

89] *I do not know what my younger daughter had done wrong. My father was there. I beat her, hitting her all over her body. I was nervous and awoke in great anxiety.*

The patient had similar dreams on various occasions. In her dreams her younger daughter was either ill or she was beating her. These are typical dreams whose meaning has been pointed out by Freud: "to beat a child" may symbolize masturbation. In the present dream the meaning is still clearer, for she is beating her younger daughter, a symbol of her genital organs. The presence of the father in the dream must be in connection with excitation derived from her oedipus complex.

90] *My daughter had gone out onto the balcony and received an electric shock from a luminous advertising sign.*

After telling her dream the patient said that it referred to a vertical luminous electric sign which she had really seen on the balcony of her brother's house. Because of its shape this dream element has a phallic symbolic value. To go out onto the balcony means to leave her introversion and go in search of external pleasures. The balcony may also symbolize the vulva. Finally, the electric shock stands for her genital excitation, which was partly provoked by the real stimulus of the phallic symbol—the vertical sign. The dream takes place on her brother's balcony because of infantile sexual experiences with him.

91] *On a table there is a large bird, a horrible pelican with slate grey feathers. This creature is a child, the daughter of my sister Susan. I do not know who else is there, but they feed it and fill its beak, which looks like clam shells. They feed it on grapes as large as cherries. I take them out of its mouth and see that the grapes had stalks and skin. I wonder at them giving that to a girl. I take out the grapes to take off the stalks and skin so as to give them to her properly. There is an ant's nest, and I throw it down.*

The elaboration of the latent thoughts behind this dream is complicated and sometimes comical. The patient is worried that people will talk about her conduct, but she reacts by telling herself that a certain amount of instinctual freedom is tolerable in a woman as long as the man concerned is worthy of her.

This interpretation was reached through her associations. She began by describing the visit of an old friend, Rose, from the country. In the course of conversation, Rose remarked that she had come to visit her sister Susan, who had left her husband and to whom she had promised some badly needed financial assistance on condition that she keep away from men. The patient considered this condition very harsh and had replied that it is not always possible to live alone. This was also her own situation.

The next association, which started the interpretation, was that the horrible bird of the dream—with slate grey feathers—

stands for Rose, who always dressed in slate grey or black and was as horrible as a bird of ill-omen because of the exacting conditions she was imposing on her sister. (A play on words in Spanish alludes to Rose's grey hair: *pelicano*, pelican; *pelo-canoso*, grey hair. On the basis of this play on words in the dream work, the patient recalled that as children she and Rose had amused themselves by playing at speaking Italian.)

The patient's sister, by a coincidence which the dream makes use of, is also called Susan, and both she and Rose's sister are represented in the dream. This Susan is a person with few sexual inhibitions.

In the dream the bird (Rose) is Susan's daughter instead of her sister as in reality. This is a reversal of the real situation, for in reality Rose adopts the attitude of a prohibiting mother, and not that of a submissive daughter, toward her sister. As frequently happens in dreams, this reversal goes hand in hand with another: in the manifest content it is Rose (the bird) and not her sister who seeks libidinal gratification, and we shall see later how this is symbolized. These changes are due to the patient's wanting, in the dream, to make Rose feel that she is not right in setting the absurd condition. Thus she puts her in her sister's place.

The libidinal gratification is represented by the following symbols: the beak-like clam shells are the female genital organ; the grapes with the stalks are the male genitals; and eating is a substitute for the genital act.

Finally, the last part of the dream stands for the conditions set by Rose; in other words, she eats "good" or "bad" things, removing everything that might have troublesome consequences in order not to provoke individual or social conflict. As to the "ants," they were found through associations to symbolize the people in the patient's environment who might criticize her conduct; this was the cause of her having to give up things that were not socially acceptable. That is to say, contrary to what happened in actual life, the pelican in the dream receives the grapes under favorable conditions, and we are led to understand that it accepts them with pleasure and without criticism.

92] *I dreamed about you. You bent down to greet me and your shirt came out on one side. I came close in order to fix it for you, and then I noticed that you were very hairy, but the hair was soft.*

This is an erotic transference dream connected with the analyst. In order to avoid censorship, the latent content makes an attempt to take on a moral aspect. The result is that the sexual closeness appears as the analyst coming to greet the patient, and as an attempt on her part to fix his shirt, which has a visible phallic symbolism. The final elements of the dream—the analyst's being "very hairy, but the hair was soft"—are connected with the patient's fantasies about the great sexual potency of the desired object, which gives her a pleasant feeling.

The following dreams include genital orgasm in the latent content. They are typical dreams which occur frequently, and they are often simple to interpret because they are accompanied by genital pleasure which is remembered on awakening.

93] *I throw myself from the top story of my house into the inner courtyard.*

94] *My daughter threw herself or fell from the balcony into the street.*

95] *I was run over by a car. I could only see the front of the bonnet.*

96] *I was running beside the train. When I began to feel sexual pleasure I awoke.*

Proceeding now to further examples, we can see how frequently genital conflict is present. For instance, a twelve-year-old girl dreams:

97] *I am on the edge of a cliff and a white horse is pursuing me. I feel my mother and father have abandoned me. I feel anxious and wake up suddenly.*

The mere translation of the symbols gives us the interpretation. We may assume that the white horse represents both her own impulses and a man who is pursuing her sexually, that the cliff is the danger of her falling (giving herself sexually), and that the parents abandoning her refers to her fantasies of freedom from the sexual restrictions of childhood. Finally, the feeling of anxiety comes from the ego which feels abandoned and overcome by instincts.

This symbolic interpretation was confirmed by the dreamer when she described the situation that gave rise to the dream. It happened when she was twelve years old, long before the interpretation was made, which explains the naiveté of the symbols used. The patient said that she had looked older than her age, so much so that during a vacation, a couple who had made her parents' acquaintance had asked them for her hand in marriage for their son, who was not with them at the time. A few days before this she had found on the dining room table a huge box of chocolates, a present from this couple, and her parents had smiled at each other significantly.

The fact that the horse was white may be an allusion to their having asked for her hand in marriage, which had surprised her but also excited her sexually, and thus caused the anxiety dream.

An analogous conflict during pre-puberty gives rise to the following dream of a woman:

98] *A man was pursuing me and a huge block of granite was falling on me. I ran and ran but could not shout.*

A symbolic interpretation shows us that the pursuit includes a sexual meaning, and that the huge block of granite represents both the penis in erection and the dangers she unconsciously associated with her sexual wishes. Consciously, in the dream, running is fleeing from pursuit, but unconsciously it also signifies sexual satisfaction.

"I could not shout" indicates that during the dream the dreamer's instinctual tendencies dominate her moral ones, for she cannot defend herself. The situation is analogous to that found in the dreams of exhibitionists, who picture themselves naked among crowds of people and unable to flee.

The dreamer accepted the interpretation, and the reference to the phallic symbol was confirmed by her association that in her school days she had often unexpectedly encountered exhibitionists. Moreover, with the huge block of granite she associated "street" and "large hole," which also spoke in favor of the interpretation given to the dream.

99] *I have a purse and my mother wants to take it from me. I try to stop her but she takes it away and then gives it back soiled.*

This was also dreamed by a woman. A purse is a well-known symbol for the female genital organ, because it can contain things. To be soiled indicates the evil moral consequences of sexual desire, but the dream work solves the conflict between instincts and morality by a projection that makes the mother responsible for what happened.

On the other hand, in the dream of another woman who is more daring in her instinctual life, the mother does not appear as the culprit but as an enemy who pursues her on account of her heterosexual activity. (In children's stories this traumatic situation is masked by making the mother a stepmother.)

100] *A tiger is pursuing my husband and me. My husband opens and shuts his umbrella to defend us.*

Thanks to the patient's associations, the tiger could be interpreted as the mother, for, one after the other, she named several older women who represented mother substitutes. The remaining element in the dream, the opening and shutting of her husband's umbrella, is a clear symbol of erection and coitus. In other words, in the dream, driven by her heterosexual desires, the woman is able to free herself from instinctual prohibitions derived from the early infantile mother-child relationship.

101] *At the table, my husband with our son in his arms and I with our daughter beside me. My husband is making jokes, gay as usual. I try to calm him, but he spills a jug of wine and I get angry. Later I am in the bathroom cleaning my mouth after eating cake.*

This is the dream of a married woman who is worried about the possibility of becoming pregnant again. Because of this she rejects her sexual desires, and this appears in the manifest content of the dream in a clearly understandable symbolization.

The woman had two children. In the dream the son in her husband's arms and the daughter beside her are symbols of the male and female genitals. Sitting at the table and eating cake represent sexual activity, which is also indicated by the husband's gaiety (a sign of excitation) and by spilling the liquid in the jug (symbolizing ejaculation). The last part of the dream is an upward displacement of the genital organs to the mouth and represents, in a disguised way, her washing her genitals in order to avoid pregnancy.

The dream work tries to present pleasant images so as to overcome the latent traumatic situation, but it does not always succeed. An old Spanish *romance* describing a dream is a good example of this. The poem tries to disguise the latent fear, but in the end the effort fails and the repressed material emerges quite clearly, probably causing the dreamer to awake in anxiety.

EL ENAMORADO Y LA MUERTE

Un sueño soñaba anoche
Soñito del alma mía,
Soñaba con mis amores,
Que en mis brazos los tenía.
Ví entrar señora tan blanca,
Muy más que la nieve fría.
Por donde has entrado, amor?
Como has entrado, mi vida?
Las puertas están cerradas,
Ventanas y celosías.
—No soy el amor, amante:
La muerte que Diós te envía.

THE LOVER AND DEATH

I dreamed last night,
Dream of my heart,
I dreamed of my love
Whom I held in my arms.
Came a lady so white,
Than the cold snow, much whiter.
How came you here, my love?
How did you enter, love of my life?
The doors are all locked,
The windows and blinds all bolted.
I am not love, lover;
I am death sent thee by God.

There are many sources of instinctual conflict during the development of a child. In our society these become associated with parental and family prohibitions which have a forceful influence upon the child. The adult must overcome a number of neurotic fears, mostly unconscious, which hinder his enjoyment of sexual life. Childhood stories reflect this psychological fact in all the dangers that the hero must overcome before being able to enter the palace of the princess. These dangers are the obstacles to emotional and physical participation in intercourse. The obstacles result largely from conflicts in early parent-child relationships. The longed-for palace of the princess is the female genital organ.

Conflicts between sexual desires and fears are frequently manifest in adults' dreams.

102] *The Allies had conquered the coast of the African continent, but now they had to penetrate into the jungle.*

X's treatise on the Panama Canal.

The day residue was the Allied landing on the African coast during the Second World War. The repressed material, which was the motive of the dream, refers to a love affair of the dreamer. He had dared to caress a woman—"the Allies had conquered the coast"—and he was thinking of the possibility of intercourse, represented in the dream by "penetrating into the jungle," i.e., entering into a female genital symbol.

The canal in the second part also represents the female genital "canal," and the treatise mentioned—stating how this canal should be handled—alludes by displacement to the social conventions that permit or prohibit intimate relations with a woman.

The dreamer has an identical conflict in another of his dreams:

103] *We were already on our summer vacation. My fiancée spoke about putting on a new bathing suit, but I answered that I could get along with the old one.*

The fiancée urges the dreamer to change his sexual conduct toward her and have intercourse, represented in the dream by putting on a new bathing suit. It was one worn by another man, whom they knew had had intimate relations with a woman; to put on such a bathing suit meant, therefore, to do as he did. His fiancée's encouragement is a reversal of the real situation, but at the same time it expresses his reaction to the excitement that she produces in him. To be on summer vacation means to him to be already married or behaving as if he was.

Sometimes the content of the dream expresses the overcoming of sexual fear:

104] *I am fearlessly plastering the walls with posters. I am carrying a great number of posters under my arm.*

The day residue was the fact of having put up revolutionary posters during a workmen's strike, which the man had done although he was frightened. The dream overcomes this fear completely. The latent meaning is to overcome sexual fear, coitus being symbolized by sticking posters on the wall with a brush. Sexual potency appears as a great quantity of posters under his arm, a substitution for his legs.

105] *I was going to meet the servant girl from downstairs. I could see the old woman from that apartment, and I was speaking to her.*

The servant in the dream represents the dreamer's genital experience with servants. It symbolizes the woman who "serves" him sexually. Therefore she appears as the servant from downstairs, i.e., his genitality. The "old woman" is his mother, who was displeased by his behavior.

106] *I could see myself with large, thick eyeglasses.*

This is the dream of a man who is discontented because of his passive and clumsy behavior with women. The eyeglasses symbolize the testicles. The dream dramatizes a vulgar Argentine expression which alludes scornfully to a man with overdeveloped glands as a man who is incapable of doing anything properly.

Another dream uses slippers (something worn on the lower part of the body) instead of glasses to express the same idea. This dream is more extensive than the previous one and describes the situation better.

107] *I was wearing some slippers which were too large for me, and they prevented me from walking.*

108] *A lion was pursuing me and I wanted to escape. I was shut up in a room and I could not find the door to get out. I felt terribly anxious.*

Dreams such as this are frequent in women who have not yet started a normal heterosexual life. An unmarried woman often has the above dream. The lion, like wild animals, monsters, or abnormal or bad people, as we have seen in other dreams, represents a sexually excited man pursuing her. She cannot escape because of her own desires.

The anxiety in the dream is provoked by the conflict between intense instinctual desire and opposing moral tendencies. It is solved to some degree by the dreamer's assuring herself that she wanted to escape but could not. Of course, it was she herself who invented the dream which revealed both her sexual desires and her fears.

On other occasions a dream of this kind may indicate frigidity. The woman wants to find in intercourse the "exit" for her excitement through orgasm, but she fails and is in anguish. Such a dream might also refer to other conflicts, such as homosexual wishes and fears.

109] *My niece was going in a streetcar with my brother. You allowed her to sit beside you for a while, but presently you made her get up.*

Going with someone (co-ire) indicates sexual activity. In the dream the psychoanalyst, as the parent substitute, allows the niece to begin in a small way, but afterwards he stops her from going further. In other words, the patient reproduces in the analytic situation the parental prohibitions regarding incestuous objects.

The younger niece symbolizes the dreamer's sexual organ. The day residue of the dream was that she had seen her niece lovingly embrace her brother, as she herself would have liked to do during childhood.

Painful dreams may be caused by the interruption of a love affair, either through the absence of the loved one or the cessation of the affection of either party. Sexual excitement then leads to frustration.

110] *Some milk which had curdled, because when I put it on to boil it was already spoiled.*

A woman dreamed this after her fiancé's departure. In Argentine slang, milk represents semen.

The two following dreams were dreamed by a man who was in conflict with his wife; when the relations between them seem to improve, the dreams take on a more pleasant aspect.

111] *The parking lot near the movie theater was illuminated. I was going up in an elevator with a lady in evening dress.*

But when he considers the real state of his marriage, his dreams are sad.

112] *The parking lot near the movie theater, but empty or badly illuminated.*

The car represents the woman he loves, and the absence of cars in the parking lot means her aloofness, or the absence of her love, or the absence of intercourse, which appears as a lack of light. In the first dream the illumination is sexual desire. Coitus appears as going up in the elevator with a lady in evening dress—she is also sexually excited.

Marriage is a decisive event in the sexual life of an adult. Social customs give it the greatest possibility for direct and sublimated erotic gratification. But external circumstances—such as economic difficulties, environmental prejudices, internal conflict, or emotional immaturity—often prevent the attainment of this gratification. Thus the thought of matrimony is often repressed, reappearing in dreams in various guises.

113] *I am sitting for an examination, and one of the professors asks me three questions which I answer very well. One of the questions is about sentences handed down by judges, which include financial responsibility.*

To sit for an examination is to examine his own capacity closely, and the number 3 indicates sexual potency. The dreamer questions whether he is potent enough to contract matrimony; this is expressed by "financial responsibility," since in matrimony one is "sentenced to a life term" and obliged to earn money to keep a wife. This was the patient's greatest worry.

114] *I had to buy something and I was doing so. Then I had to register what I had bought. All this was connected with Love.*

"Love" is the surname of a person with whom the dreamer has business connections. Because of this particular name, this day residue is taken advantage of in the dream in connection with his love affair. In the dream the man must get a woman—"buy something"—and marry her, i.e., register what he has bought in the Registry Office. All this must be done with love.

115] *I am going into my house; while I go from one room to another, the walls begin to fall down.*

It is the conjugal home that falls to pieces, because of the dreamer's unhappy experiences with her husband.

Some dreams have a similar manifest content and this corresponds to similar latent meaning. Typical dreams of this type are examination dreams, dreams of missing a train, and dreams of convenience.

One group of typical examination dreams has special characteristics: the dream depicts as unsuccessful an examination that was previously passed successfully, the dreamer thus having to go through it again with greater difficulties. Thus a doctor dreams:

116] *I still have to pass one or several examinations in the university in order to become a doctor.*

These dreams are frequent in people with inhibitions of various kinds and who consciously or unconsciously consider themselves incapable of leading a mature genital life. (See DREAM 113.) Their incapacity is expressed in the dream by the fact that they have not yet passed the examinations allowing them to practice professionally, i.e., as adult men and women, because professional practice in the dream is a displacement from genital activity. Sexual anxiety appears in the dreams as examination anxiety. Thus, in the doctor's dream, to be a doctor means to have strong sexual potency. The patient lacked confidence because he had been circumcised and also severely threatened and restricted in his childhood.

In the following dream the relationship between a professional examination and genitality is quite clear.

117] *My father tells me that if I do not pass my B.A. examination I shall not be able to marry George.*

A woman dreamed this shortly before her marriage. She doubted her instinctual capacity, which appears as anxiety about her B.A. exam. The father is her super-ego, or psychoanalyst, telling her that she cannot marry unless her genital response is normal.

118] *Somebody was telling me I had to do sixth grade again, and I answered that that referred to someone else, not to me.*

Like the previous dream, this is also the dream of a woman expressing doubt about her genitality. She refers to the sixth grade because, according to her associations, girls of twelve and thirteen are in this class, this being the age when girls turn into women. "Sixth" grade also alludes to "sex." To do the sixth grade again means that she is not yet a woman; it also means continuing with her love affair, during which she had started to have sexual relations, which, however, left her unsatisfied because of her frigidity.

She is calmed in the dream by projecting the painful element onto her sister, who is the other person referred to in the dream, and who had had, in actual fact, to repeat her examinations. It should also be borne in mind that the younger sister is a symbol for the female genital organ.

Dreams of missing a train or not being able to take it are also typical. In the majority of cases in my experience, I have found them to mean that the dreamer is missing the erotic opportunities offered by life, because of his inhibitions.

119] *In my home town. I am in the same state of anxiety at finding myself there as in other similar dreams. I am with my female cousins on horseback. I tell them that I must take a train or airplane to Buenos Aires, and I am worried because I fear I shall be short of money.*

To be in his home town is to recognize his neurosis, originating in childhood, which causes anxiety. His cousins were forbidden childhood libidinous objects. This corresponds to an actual situation of sexual fear regarding a certain woman.

The horse symbolizes his penis by association with a riddle he had heard in childhood. To go on horseback is to be sexually excited toward his cousins. But it also indicates a homosexual attitude toward his father, on whose lap he played at horses as a little boy; this game gave him a ticklish feeling around his arms, while at the same time he tried to feel his father's penis with his knee. This homosexual attitude, still consciously active, prevents him from approaching women. To come to Buenos Aires is to initiate psychoanalytic treatment, but he doubts whether his potency will allow him to reach sexual normality.

In Portuguese, "to be left with the bags" means to remain

with sad thoughts. A Brazilian patient explained the meaning of this expression to me, and in the following dream, missing the train on which his bags had been put has the meaning of avoiding death, which coincides with Freud's remarks about dreams of missing trains * but is opposed to the meaning we have indicated up to now for this type of dream. This diversity may be reconciled by the fact that to travel by train symbolizes in the dream a relationship with a specific person which could result in either love or death, depending on the gratifying or frustrating characteristics of the relationship. The patient's mother is already dead. He feels that she severely curbed his sexual freedom, i.e., "drove him to the position of dealing death to his instincts."

120] *I had to catch a train which left at eight o'clock, or ten minutes past eight, and my mother was on it. I had already sent my luggage. I was going to the station and thought it was already late, but that I would lose more time if I tried to get a taxi to travel two blocks. I also thought that if I took a taxi I could get to the next station. A boy was telling me that I would not arrive in time as it was already 8:20. Even so, I thought I would take the next train and that my mother would wait for me in Santa Asunción [where his mother is buried].*

The dream clearly indicates that to take the train is to go to the place where his mother is buried, which to the patient means to go on being subjected to her. He associated Santa Asunción with the name of a railway station, with the Virgin, chastity, and heaven; he finally decided that his mother would wait there without his being in too much of a hurry to join

* ". . . dreams of missing the train . . . They are consolation dreams, directed against another anxiety perceived in dreams—the fear of death. 'To depart' is one of the most frequent and one of the most readily established death symbols. The dream therefore says consolingly: 'Reassure yourself, you are not going to die (to depart) . . .' " (*The Interpretation of Dreams*. The Dream Work.)

her. In other words, the dream refers to his conflicts about emancipating himself from his mother.

The numbers in the dream refer to ages when he was either very close to or far from his mother. Thus eight plus twenty equals twenty-eight, the age when he freed himself from his family by getting married. Two blocks was the distance he was allowed to wander from his home during childhood. The boy represents the conflict between the impulse to be a dependent child reunited with his mother or an independent adult separated from her.

Other typical dreams are dreams of convenience. Generally, these are interpreted too quickly by giving them the meaning which appears in the manifest content. According to my experience, they are not pleasurable but very masochistic, and the apparent satisfaction has the value only of a comforting façade that screens an internal submissiveness. Such dreams are frequent, for example, in enuretics who are often intensely masochistic.

A patient is awakened one morning, Monday, May 24, to go to work. He goes on sleeping and dreams:

121] *I could see the dates—May 24 and 25 were marked red on the calendar as if both days were holidays.* [*In the Argentine, May 25 is a holiday.*]

This is a dream of convenience; had the first date been a holiday, he could have gone on sleeping. But as an antecedent to the dream: the previous Sunday one of his checks had been marked "insufficient funds" and returned to him. As he was given no explanation for it, he thought that perhaps someone had forged a check and taken all his money from the bank. He proposed to verify this the following day, Monday the 24th. He forgot to do so and arrived at the bank at the last minute, but there he committed another symptomatic action by forgetting the credit slip which indicated his name, signature, and the amount of money in his account. The dreamer himself interpreted it, like his fantasy of the previous day, as a masochistic wish to have his money taken away from him.

In other words, this is the principal motive of his dream, during which he went on sleeping, apparently peacefully, but in reality enjoying the pain caused by the loss of his money.

A more pleasurable motive was his fear that his wife might be pregnant. With the date in red, he associated menstruation, which it would have pleased him to see in his wife. We can deduce from this that the loss of the money in the bank symbolized the loss of his wife's pregnancy, i.e., her miscarriage.

122] *I wish to have intercourse with my wife, but before agreeing she starts carrying out some of her rituals. This annoys me, and my erection ends.*

Associations proved this to be a dream of convenience. The dreamer himself is symbolized in the dream by his penis, and the erection which ends is his not "getting up" to go to work at an earlier hour than usual, which, according to new regulations which annoyed him, he should have done. This is represented by the wife's rituals; but the rituals are also his own, in waking up, and since he thinks them improper for a man, so in his dream he ascribes them to his wife.

Dreams are like old silent films without sound or color. My experience shows that *the real common denominator in colored dreams is the existence of repressed anal excremental contents.*

This anal excremental meaning of colored dreams becomes clearly apparent when the dominant color is brown, and if before such dreams the dreamers have had anxiety-provoking experiences in connection with anality.

Such is the case of a young woman at the time when she was just starting a heterosexual genital relationship. She had the following dream after having carried out anal intercourse for the first time:

123] *Mother told me she could not find my light summer shoes which I wanted, but that instead she had found some beautiful brown ones.*

In this dream the mother represented the psychoanalyst and also the dreamer herself, developing her genital activity in an identification with her mother in her psychoanalytic sessions. The two kinds of shoes in the dream were symbols for her perineal organs, the light ones corresponding to the vagina and the brown ones to the rectum and anus, both as organs which receive the penis. The first pair were summer shoes because anal intercourse seemed cold to the dreamer compared with vaginal intercourse. And summer or summer resorts in dreams often represent genitality, perhaps because genital excitement elicits a feeling of warmth and well-being.

The patient had other dreams during the same night with the latent content of anal intercourse, which confirmed the anal meaning of the dream with the brown shoes, for dreams of the same night deal with the same repressed latent contents.

Colored dreams springing from anxiety-provoking anal experiences are not necessarily in brown. Thus an individual had the following dream with other colors the night after he submitted to his mistress's whim of caressing and licking each other's anus and introducing a finger into it. The fact that the woman forced the patient to such practices made him consider her as phallic and destructive toward him.

124] *A well-bound book. It was a colored dream.*

The manifest aspect of the dream arose from having been forced to listen to a woman read a poor scientific paper the day before, and his submission to this woman symbolized his subjection to his mistress's "poor" genital habits. The patient also felt it a bother to have to submit to his personal analysis as part of his psychoanalytic training.

The book in the dream, which referred to the poor scientific paper, was well bound. This manifest element of the dream soothed him in opposition to the other feared latent content: that his mistress would damage his anus.

These dreams came from the previous day's painful anal practices. More often colored dreams do not have such direct antecedents, although they are found to be connected with excremental anal contents.

A further example of a colored dream is that of another woman patient. She dreamed it after an unhappy love affair which led her to reject her genitality and make an instinctive regression to anality. This woman often had fantasies of anal intercourse, which she considered a masochistic subjection to male phallic aggression. Her lover had tried to leave her. The need to detach herself from him appeared in the dream as vomiting a pencil. In the latent content this represented defecating the lover's penis. During her psychoanalytic treatment she had increased her resistance and had unconscious fantasies of changing her analyst for another, with the aim of returning to her oedipal objects.

125] *I was at the window of my inner hall. I was trying to vomit three colored crayons. I was taking a blue pencil to vomit a violet one.*

Repeating her unconscious thought, in her dream this woman tried to free herself from her lover and replace him by another man. The penises of both were represented by the differently colored crayons, which referred to their different characteristics. Through a play on words, "violet" also meant "violation." At one moment in the dream there were three pencils, owing to the phallic symbolism this number has. The window of the inner hall represented both her vagina and her anus.

The anal excremental contents that caused this last dream to be in colors came up very clearly during the patient's associations. Thus she connected the colored crayons with Plasticene and other materials used for coloring, which have clearly anal excremental characteristics. She also qualified her behavior with the two men as "dirty rinsing," calling herself a "filthy bitch" afterwards.

Some of the above dreams show that latent anal excremental contents, from which manifest colors arise, often do not appear clearly in the associations. They are masked by genital contents and sometimes even by oral-digestive ones, as these thoughts provoke less conscious rejection than anal contents.

This applies to a male patient who had a masochistic

colored dream about genital castration. This dream seemed to be adequately interpreted on the basis of this content. But the inexplicable fact that the dream was in colors made me insist on further associations. The patient then remembered another dream of the same night. Forgotten dreams often give us important clues, and this one defined the castratory aggression as urethral and excremental in character; it also disclosed the identity of the castrating person.

The dream had been caused by the man's thoughts about his approaching marriage, which had increased his genital fears of impotence. In another dream reflecting the same fear, he had to sit for an examination he was not sure he would pass successfully. In still another, he was playing golf and lost a ball while trying to drive it into a hole. The patient's dream was:

126] *A circus; it was a colored dream.*

He associated this manifest content with a circus tent in the city where he had spent his puberty. At that age he used to go out with girls, but without daring to have any genital activity. He remembered having witnessed a boxing match in the circus tent, during which one of the boxers' shorts began slipping down; when the boxer put his hands down to keep them from falling, his opponent gave him a knockout blow. When I insisted on still more associations, as the presence of colors had yet to be interpreted, the patient remembered another dream of the same night:

127] *It was like being in a bathroom. It was very beautiful; I was bathing. A naked person came in, throwing cold water on me. He had a small box from which water spouted. He wanted to fight me, but I grabbed his little box and in turn threw cold water at him with it. So I managed to drive him away.*

In the course of his associations to this dream, he interpreted that the person he drove away was his mother. She had always opposed his marriage, and now that she realized that he was terrified by its imminence, she criticized him for it all the more.

The dreamer's subjection to his mother also appeared in the first dream, where the circus tent symbolized the maternal womb, i.e., his mother surrounding him and depriving him of genital freedom.

After the patient's associations it became evident that "throwing water from a small box" symbolized his mother's aggressions against him. It was as if his mother were urinating and defecating on his marriage to destroy it. The patient's associations expressed these contents very clearly. For example, he said that the other person in the dream had the small box in front of his belly, as if it were a penis, although the "small box" seemed to him more like the female genital organ, and, since it held liquid, the bladder.

As is often the case, in the last part of his dream the patient attempted to get rid of his anxiety by doing actively with his phallic mother what he had suffered from her passively.

The dream also arose out of the patient's fantasies of having sexual intercourse with women other than his fiancée. Consciously, these fantasies had the aim of overcoming his castration fears, but more deeply they were an attempt to avoid his fiancée, with whom he no longer had genital contact. It became apparent in the dream interpretation that, apart from his mother, the other person in the dream also represented his fiancée, who was a feared mother substitute. Thus in his associations he remembered having gone to a railway station with a friend of his fiancée's in order to make a trip with her, and then having to leave her there because he had diarrhea. In this association the regressive excremental anal contents reappeared. These contents were the source of the colors in the dream about the circus.

Repressed psychic contents that are not manifest excremental anal ones, but are derived from them, may also give rise to colored dreams. Contents such as these are, for instance, corpses, money, anal sadism, or anal masochism.

The theory that colored dreams have their origin in repressed anal excremental contents is supported to a certain extent by the psychoanalytic hypothesis that painting is a sublimation of anal instincts. The origin of painting, as smearing with excrements, becomes apparent above all in the psychoanalytic treatment of children.

Studies on ornamentation and the origin of clothes have led me to assume that the first paintings were those of primitive mothers on their newborn. They consisted in smearing their bodies with excrement and urine. Though we would now call it "dirty," this was done with the magic purpose of preserving the condition the children had in their mothers' wombs, believing that this covering was a protection. Primitive mothers may have acquired this idea following the nature of their own biology, since *inter urinam et faeces nascimur.*

The first human tattoo must also have been like this, just as the first clothing must have consisted in covering the newborn infant with fetal membranes. Later on, painting was displaced from tattooing on the human body to external objects. Excrements and urine were followed by other painting materials, some of which are even today analogous to anal excrement, reminiscent of their origin.

Colored dreams are like painted dreams. Sometimes, when hearing a patient describe his dreams, we have the impression that these had a first version in black and white to which the dreamer added color in order to instill into them their anal excremental meaning.

Chapter 6

THE TRAUMATIC SITUATION IN THE GENESIS OF DREAMS

According to Freud, dreams are the gratification of unconscious wishes. This psychoanalytic concept does not conflict with masochistic dreams, anxiety dreams, or dreams that represent punishment by the super-ego. Nevertheless, there is one type of dream that seems to be an exception—dreams of traumatic neuroses. When a deep psychological shock has been suffered, the dreams which follow it are a monotonous reproduction of the unpleasant sensations experienced at the time of the trauma.

There are other exceptions. Forgotten unpleasant experiences of the subject's childhood which had a traumatic influence on his psychic evolution can frequently be discerned in dreams. If dreams often reproduce these infantile traumatic experiences, this also contradicts the theory of wish-fulfillment, though not completely, for in these dreams the infantile traumatic situation is often modified and turned toward wish-fulfillment.

Freud did not believe that the exception proves the rule. According to him, the most that can be said is that an exception does not invalidate the rule. Bearing in mind the exceptions we have mentioned, where the alleged function of a dream is not fulfilled, Freud introduced a slight modification in psychoanalytic theory. Instead of saying that a dream is the gratification of wishes, he says that a dream is *an attempt to gratify wishes.*

In my opinion the traumatic situation plays a part not only in the dreams of traumatic neuroses and in those reproducing certain infantile traumatic situations, but in all dreams. I believe that the existence of a traumatic situation is a very important factor in the genesis of dreams, possibly the most important factor.

When we study a subject's dreams we are impressed by the frequency of unpleasant contents. As Freud mentioned, this was observed as far back as 1891 by Debacker, when he studied children's dreams, and by Weed and Hallam in 1895, in connection with adults' dreams. According to these authors, 58 per cent of all adults' dreams are unpleasant. This is not in itself an absolute contradiction to wish-fulfillment theory, for unpleasant dreams may be found, after interpretation, to represent the gratification of wishes; the existence in the personality of instincts that are unpleasant to the ego, the intervention of masochism, and the existence of the super-ego could explain the apparent contradiction.

But this explanation does not quite satisfy me. It would seem that, even making allowances for the above-mentioned motives, the frequency of the unpleasant character of dreams is not entirely explained. The study and interpretation of our own dreams and those of others lead to the impression that the dream is attracted toward disagreeable or painful things.

A patient told me the following fantasy, at a point in his treatment when masochism was frequently manifest: "A man secretly breaks into my sister's room and rapes her. I discover him, fight with him, and overpower him. I knock him down and crush his skull with the heel of my shoe." Then the patient asked: "Is this a sadistic or a masochistic fantasy?" He had no doubt that the analyst would confirm his sadism;

he liked to think of himself as a sadist, whereas his masochism was distasteful to him.

I replied: "In your fantasy of crushing the other man's skull, your activity was sadistic; but since the source of your thoughts was the fantasy in which you imagined your sister to be raped, and as you identify with her and with the rapist, the fantasy must be considered more masochistic than sadistic." I believe that this also happens in dreams; the more or less intense gratification of wishes screens the unpleasant situations to which the dreamer is subjected, and which must be included as a source of the dream.

Another strange phenomenon is related to the theory of wish-fulfillment. This is the frequency with which instinctual gratification in dreams lacks intensity. Dreams tend to be cowardly in attaining gratification. An example will help clarify what we call *the cowardice of dreams.* During his psychoanalytic treatment a patient dreams:

128] *I kiss Aurea.*

By association he tells me that this concerns a young woman he met at X, and with whom he would have liked to become intimate, and could have done so had he been a little more enterprising. The girl, whom he had visited on several occasions, had offered only slight resistance to his advances. But he lacked courage. During treatment the patient blamed himself for his past conduct.

With the help of the patient's associations, it is easy to explain the genesis of the dream. In the dream the patient corrects a past situation which hurt his pride and was therefore disagreeable; he turned it into a pleasant situation by daring to kiss the girl. But why does the patient only venture to dream of a kiss, when his associations show clearly that he wanted more intimate contact? Why does he not dream, for instance, that Aurea is his mistress? The patient is almost as unenterprising in his dream as he was in actual fact.

Let us suppose that the reason for his actual shyness toward Aurea was caused by a neurotic inhibition produced in him by this young woman whom he unconsciously associated with his mother. We can then explain the lack of intense instinctual satisfaction by this connection with the oedipus complex. But why does he not dare to create a dream which would destroy his inhibitions by making Aurea completely different from his mother, which would permit him to have a happy and complete love affair with her?

We find the same element in any other dream. For instance, another patient had a dream one night after masturbating.

129] *I have banged myself and knocked out a tooth. The teeth next to it become loose and move. I show my fiancée a flame. She becomes uneasy, but I remain calm.*

The masturbation had given rise to intense castration fear, which in the dream is overcome in two ways: first, by displacement—the loss of one or several teeth is never as dreadful as castration; and second, by projecting his anxiety onto his fiancée—in the dream, his fiancée, and not the patient himself, is upset by the fire (sexual excitement). But even so, in this supposedly soothing dream, the patient admits both the loss of a tooth and his anxiety. Why does he not achieve even greater satisfaction of his wishes by dreaming, for instance, that there is nothing wrong with him, and that if there is a fire it does not destroy anything, and that no one feels anxiety? Of course, it can always be said that the intervention of the super-ego wanting to punish the ego for masturbating, prevents complete satisfaction. But in my opinion, a fixation on the disagreeable ideas giving rise to the dream also intervenes.

Many more examples could be found, but I shall limit myself to two. First, the first dream to be published with a psychoanalytic interpretation: Freud's dream about "Irma's injection."

Otto, a friend of Freud's, one day gives him unpleasant news about the condition of one of Freud's patients, Irma. Freud believes he detects in his friend's words veiled reproaches about his medical handling of the case. During the night Freud has an incomprehensible dream. He interprets it and concludes that it represents the gratification of wishes because it nullifies any possible reproaches. In the dream Irma's illness continues because she has not followed Freud's advice properly, and also because Otto has given her an injection badly. It also appears in the dream that Irma's ailments are not psychogenic in origin, and therefore Freud is not to blame for having failed to cure her by psychological treatment.

Freud writes, "It is as though Otto had said to me, 'You do not take your medical duties seriously enough; you are not conscientious; you do not keep your promise.' Thereupon this train of thought placed itself at my service, in order that I might give proof of my extreme conscientiousness, of my intimate concern about the health of my relatives, friends, and patients. Curiously enough, there are also some painful memories in this material which confirm the blame attached to Otto, rather than to my own exculpation . . . the wish to be innocent of Irma's illness . . ." If the basis of this dream is the fear of having been somewhat negligent professionally in Irma's treatment, why does he not dare attain complete satisfaction of his wishes in the dream? Why does he not dream, for instance, that the treatment had excellent results, that Irma is in better health than ever, and that everyone admires him for his success?

The dream gives the impression that Freud did not feel strong enough to reject the reproaches he believed he had sensed in his friend's words. It is as though the dream accumulated excuses without seriously believing any of them. This is in complete agreement with what Freud wrote about the interpretation of his dream: "The whole plea—for this dream is nothing else—recalls vividly the defense offered by a man who was accused by his neighbor of having returned a kettle in a damaged condition. In the first place, he said, he had returned the kettle undamaged; in the second place, it already had holes in it when he borrowed it; and in the third place, he had never borrowed it at all." Anyone listening to this man's defense would have no hesitation in declaring him guilty of damaging the kettle. His words are a clear confirmation of what they intend to deny. The defense is bad precisely because the man is convinced of his guilt and is not strong enough to free himself from this traumatic situation. Freud's defense in the dream of Irma's injection must be similarly interpreted.

The other dream demonstrating a fixation on disagreeable ideas was published under the title "Fragments of Analysis in a Case of Hysteria," and was dreamed by one of Freud's patients, Dora. Freud gives a complete interpretation of this dream, with the mastery of true genius, and everyone interested in the interpretation of dreams should read it. But with regard to the theme we are discussing here, it is only important to remember that the dream was a reaction to an unhappy love affair with a Mr. K, with whom Dora was very much in love. Grieved by her disappointment, Dora relives in her dream a period of her childhood when she had nocturnal enuresis and her father used to lift her out of bed before the accident could happen. Therefore, in the dream, escaping from the present disagreeable situation (her unhappy love affair), she seeks refuge in her father's love to prevent anything unpleasant from happening. But why does the dream not dare to change the present situation by denying, for instance, the existence of the unhappy love affair?

In all the dreams cited, a disagreeable psychic situation gives rise to the dream. In the dream of "kissing Aurea," the disagreeable situation is the subject's failure, for intrapsychic reasons, to win her love; in the dream of the man showing fire to his fiancée, there is fear of castration; in the dream of Irma's injection, there is the fear of not having conducted the patient's treatment properly; and in Dora's dream, the disappointment about the man she loved. These disagreeable situations are the starting points for the dreams.

A situation which the subject finds disagreeable, and which the dream tries to correct, is to be found at the root of the dream. This may be described as a disagreeable situation, an anxiety-provoking situation, a situation of psychic conflict, or a traumatic situation. Bearing in mind a definition of Freud's, I think the most adequate term seems to be *traumatic situation.* Indeed, Freud gives the name *trau-*

matic experience to an experience which produces in a short span of time such an intensity of psychic stimuli that the subject cannot ward them off or revise them in the usual way. These are the characteristics of the unpleasant situations which give rise to dreams, i.e., the inability of the subject to rid himself of stimuli which are too intense, or to work through them in the normal fashion.

The study of certain dreams leaves little doubt that *traumatic situation* is the best expression to use. It is clearly the case, for instance, in the following dreams of F, who, upon coming home one day, learned that his wife had eloped with a family friend. He came to the realization that, even before the elopement, an intimate relationship must have existed between them. Deeply depressed, he left his job and the country in which he lived and returned by boat to his homeland. Several days previously, his wife and her lover had also undertaken the same journey, and also by boat.

Psychoanalytic treatment lasted only a short while and remained unfinished. F suffered from a not very deep-seated neurosis, one of the symptoms of which was a somewhat premature ejaculation. His wife was much more neurotic than he, and their difficulties stemmed more from her than from him. The husband, however, because of his quick ejaculation, considered himself sexually inadequate and felt responsible for his wife's desertion. In his depressed state he worried about what people would think of him when they heard what his wife had done.

He had made great sacrifices in order to marry. It was therefore surprising to find that his depression lifted when, in the course of treatment, in reliving his wife's former behavior, he realized that her sexual difficulties were greater than his. When he reached this point in the analysis, the patient lost interest in the treatment and returned, reassured, to the country from which he had come. Nothing was heard from him again, and no attempt was made to evaluate the efficacy of the treatment. He had sought out psychoanalytic treatment in order to rid himself of neurotic personality traits which had led him, among other things, to marry a person unworthy of him.

I have already noted that, in his depressed state, F was preoccupied with what people would think when they saw him alone; also, he would have liked to live with his wife again. This situation, replete with conflicts, is elaborated in the dreams that follow.

130] *With my wife again; I ask her if she wants to marry me. She wants to know whether it will last long.* A *fellow student is present.*

To marry means to have sexual relations, and to "last long" refers to his premature ejaculation. As for the fellow student, F recalled that they used to go out together looking for women, and that at such times his sexual behavior was normal. The introduction of this memory into the dream represents the patient's answer to his wife's question. It is as if he had told her that before he married her he was sexually normal. What he does not mention in the dream is that this normality did not exist under all circumstances.

F and his fellow student sometimes had sexual relations with the same woman. With this new association the patient presented another series of thoughts which could not be analyzed.

131] *At* X, *in the garden of my home. My mother is there and also my wife and a neighbor. There is a lot of linen—women's clothes—washed and hung up to dry.*

X is the place where F resided. To wash women's linen means to remove the spots, that is, to do away with his wife's improper behavior. The patient realized that the dream reproduces the expression "to wash dirty linen in private." The linen "washed and hung up to dry" means the resolution of the marital conflict. This is shown in the patient's associations to the neighbor in the dream. Unaware of what had happened, the neighbor had recently asked the patient's wife if she would take something to her daughter, who lived in X. His wife agreed to do this, as if she were returning to the marital home, and did not tell the neighbor the real situation.

To sum up, by joining together the various partial interpretations, the dream means: "My wife returns to live with me. No one knows what has happened, and everything is settled."

The following is F's third dream:

132] *My brother is in a rowboat on the river, gathering goods that have been stolen from him. There are people watching us, and my brother makes a speech explaining what has happened.*

The stolen goods represent the stolen wife, and the rowboat, the boat on which his wife and her lover departed. Thus the dream centers on the themes that are actually troubling the patient. But to reassure the dreamer, the dream utilizes a displacement, so that in the manifest content it is not his wife but goods belonging to his brother which are stolen. The people whose opinion he fears are also reassured by means of his brother's speech. All this may constitute the gratification of wishes in the dream. To effect the displacement, the patient makes use of an actual fact: his brother and his wife are also separated, and she, like his own wife, behaved badly. The dream is now comprehensible, as is its reassuring effect on the patient.

These three dreams represent three different ways in which the subject tries to resolve his conflict. In the first dream he persuades his wife to come back and live with him; in the second he settles the situation in the privacy of his own home, without strangers knowing anything about it; in the third it is his brother and not himself who has the conflict and must solve it. (The brother might also be a symbol for his penis.) These three different mechanisms are used for the purpose of diminishing anxiety.

It is a case of depression. Like all these cases, it is originated by aggressive desires directed against a loved one and secondarily turned against the ego. In this particular case, aggression was unconsciously directed against the wife, whose conduct left so much to desire. The patient's guilt feelings impeded his aggression and sexuality from being directed toward the external object, and turned them against himself. This is why F had premature ejaculation and reproached himself and not his wife.

The wife's desertion was a traumatic situation to which the patient reacted with intense feeling that he was unable to master, and that brought about a psychogenic depression. The patient believed that he was responsible for her leaving him, and he felt that he was not able to resolve the situation. These are the characteristics of a *traumatic situation*. The other terms —disagreeable situation, anxiety-laden situation, or situation of conflict—are less appropriate designations for these psychological phenomena.

Admitting the existence of a traumatic situation as the basis of dreams is completely in accord with other psychoanalytic findings. The patient's fixation on one or several traumatic situations always proves to be at the root of his neurotic symptoms, and the analogy existing between dreams and neurotic symptoms is already known to us. On the other hand, we do not contradict the theory of wish-fulfillment by admitting the existence of a fixation on a traumatic situation in dreams. On the contrary, this extends it by pointing out an essential fact which must be taken into account in the interpretation; in other words, it strengthens the theory rather than invalidating it. If we compare the latent content with the manifest content of dreams, we can see that, except in dreams of traumatic neurosis, the traumatic situation constituting the basis of the latent content is transformed in the manifest content into a pleasant situation, or at least one which is not so unpleasant. This means that in the elaboration of the dream there has been a clear evolution *toward* the gratification of the wish.

The existence of a fundamental traumatic situation explains the dream's cowardice with regard to wish fulfillment. Dreams are not capable of venturing very far toward gratification, because the subject is psychically fixed to the traumatic situation. Were it not for this fixation, wish fulfillment would be very much more complete.

In my opinion, the traumatic situation is the principal factor in dreams and, as will be seen in the following chapter, is also one reason why thoughts take a regressive path and leave the abstract terms of ordinary thought to create concrete hallucinations. As for traumatic neuroses, there is no doubt at all that in these cases the traumatic situation is the origin of dreams. The satisfied wish is not the cause of the hallucinatory regression but only an attempt to diminish the mental discomfort brought about by a fixation on the traumatic situation.

My conception of the genesis of dreams may be simply illustrated with the help of a few paragraphs from a children's story book in which a dream is described. The dreamer is Babar, king of the elephants. After a dreadful day during which his kingdom was threatened time and again, Babar was able to fall asleep, and while deeply asleep he had the following dream [FIGURE 47]:

"I hear knocking at the door and a voice cries out: 'I am Misfortune, I have come to visit you with some of my friends.' I look through the window and see a horrible old woman surrounded by ugly white animals. Just as I am about to shout at them to go away, I stop, because I can hear sweet sounds, like birds singing. Then I see some graceful winged elephants approaching, who chase away Misfortune and bring Happiness with them."

When Babar awakes he feels better. What is the genesis of his dream? Its beginning shows us how it comes from a fixation on a traumatic situation. Indeed, the previous day troubles beyond his control menaced his kingdom. Under the influence of these ominous events, Babar, at night, sees a kind of repetition of these traumatic events dramatized in the dream as Misfortune and her friends. This is what brings about the hallucination, i.e., the dream.

The dream process continues however, and Babar, in order to diminish unpleasant psychic tension, imagines a successful fight against adversity. In the manifest content this is dramatized by the winged elephants who overcome Misfortune. This final part is only wishful thinking, and we understand that this in itself is not sufficient to generate a dream.

Of the two parts of the dream, the last and more agreeable part is the more likely to remain conscious. It is probable that the ego will manage to suppress the first part. Let us suppose that this is the case, and that on awakening from his nocturnal hallucination King Babar remembers only the part about the victorious elephants. The dream will then appear to be mere wish fulfillment which, though true, does not explain the genesis of the dream nor the reason for the hallucination.

In interpreting dreams an attempt should always be made to find the basic traumatic situation (or situations), always bearing in mind the patient's psychology and the fact that a wish that could be pleasurable to a normal individual might be traumatic to a neurotic.

A dream arises from one or several traumatic situations. A traumatic situation may in turn revive an analogous one, belonging to the patient's past experience. This happens, for instance, in Dora's dream, which we mentioned before. The current traumatic situation is her disappointing love affair with Mr. K, reviving an analogous situation in her childhood caused by nocturnal enuresis. The wish fulfillment applies to the infantile traumatic situation: in her dream Dora hallucinates her father at her bedside, as he used to be when she was a child and he came to her to prevent her wetting the bed—the infantile and regressive antecedent of vaginal lubrication. The dream clearly describes the characteristic of a traumatic situation—the subject's inability to resolve it unaided. Dora must get her father's help in her dream because she thinks she is incapable of handling the situation. The gratification of wishes in the dream consists of obtaining her father's help by reviving her infantile love for him.

We can now consider our findings and arrive at the following conclusions:

1. Dreams spring from one or more disagreeable situations which the subject is unable to master or work through nor-

mally, and which, using Freud's terminology, we call *traumatic situations*.

2. In the dream the subject has a psychic fixation on these traumatic situations.

3. Dreams are generally successful attempts to overcome the displeasure brought about by traumatic situations.

4. The attempt to overcome displeasure is effected through wish fulfillment.

5. The hallucinatory aspect of dreams is due to the influence of traumatic situations and not to the influence of the wishes they gratify.

Chapter 7

THE GENESIS OF DREAM HALLUCINATION

In the previous chapter I have shown that wish fulfillment is not only characteristic of dreams but is to be found, according to psychoanalytic theory, at the root of every psychological phenomenon, whether normal or pathological. The "distorted" fulfillment of wishes characterizes not only dreams but also perverse and neurotic symptoms. Dreams are different from the latter wish fulfillments by their hallucinatory aspect. In other words, hallucination is characteristic of dreams, in the same way as "conversion" is of hysterical symptoms, and orgiastic organization around a partial instinct is of perversions. Therefore a theory about the genesis of dreams must include a reason for the hallucinations. I shall try to provide one in this chapter by examining psychoanalytically various kinds of hallucination.

A mental image is either stimulated by an actual external object or it is an intrapsychic product. The mental image of a house, for example, is caused either by a visual perception or by the representation of one in fantasy. The ability to distinguish external reality from the products of the imagination is indispensable for the correct orientation of behavior. In other words, we must know how to distinguish the images of the house we see from the house we fantasy.

We must therefore establish certain differences between exogenous and endogenous images. Applying this distinction to images is called "reality testing," and we call the image proceeding from an external stimulus *real*, and that which proceeds from the internal stimulus of thoughts or fantasies *unreal*.

It is not possible to differentiate endogenous and exogenous images by differences in the intensity of perception, for some weak and confused stimuli from the external world may nevertheless be easily distinguished from others of internal origin which are far clearer. According to Freud, the ego tests the reality of a perception * and learns to distinguish between the two types, taking as a basis their duration and especially the possibility of reacting by escape. For example, the ego can avoid the external perception of a threat of injury by avoiding the injurious object, whereas inner perceptions such as hunger and sadness give the ego no such possibility of escape. So it can be said that this capacity to avoid things which are perceived is of fundamental importance to the ego in distinguishing the external or internal origin of perceptions: this is the basis of reality testing.

Freud writes of this mechanism: "In an earlier passage we claimed that the still helpless organism had the capacity for making a first orientation in the world by means of its perceptions, distinguishing both 'outer' and 'inner' according to their relation to actions of the muscles. A perception which is made to disappear by motor activity is recognized as external, as reality: where such activity makes no difference, the perception originates within the subject's own body—it is not real." As we have already shown, the ego can avoid the exogenous perception of a prick on the hand by the muscular action of withdrawing the hand in time; but it cannot avoid the perception of hunger or sadness, which are of internal origin.

In the other passage to which Freud refers in the above paragraph, he says: "We have now obtained material necessary for discriminating between stimuli of instinctual origin and the other (physiological) stimuli which operate on our minds. First,

* "Perception" as used here includes both exogenous and endogenous perceptions.

a stimulus of instinctual origin does not arise in the outside world but from within the organism itself. For this reason it has a different mental effect and different actions are necessary in order to remove it. Further, all that is essential in an external stimulus is contained in the assumption that it acts as a single impact, so that it can be discharged by a single appropriate action—a typical instance being that of motor flight from the source of stimulation. An instinct, on the other hand, never acts as a momentary impact but always as a constant force. As it makes its attack not from without but from within the organism, it follows that flight cannot avail against it."

In short, according to Freud, "The antithesis of the ego—nonego (outer), i.e., subject-object, is, as we have already said, thrust upon the individual at an early stage, by the experience that it can abolish external stimuli by means of muscular action, but is defenseless against those stimuli that originate in instinct." *

My observations have led me to the opposite conclusion: that the ego considers perceptions to be of internal origin when they can be successfully rejected and considers those it cannot avoid to originate outside. This statement may at first sight seem devoid of all rational foundation; nevertheless, there are psychological facts that make it seem probable and that, moreover, help to explain otherwise inexplicable psychological phenomena, such as hallucinations in dreams.

---

* The capacity to avoid an external stimulus through rejection or actual flight is also to be found in the psyche—independently from the actual flight—in the face of perceptions from the outer world. Freud expressed his idea as follows: "This function of orientating the individual in the world by discrimination between inner and outer must now, after detailed dissection of the mental apparatus, be ascribed to the system Cs (Pcpt) alone. Cs must have at its command motor innervation which determines whether the perception can be made to disappear or whether it proves persistent. The capacity for testing reality need be nothing more than this function" (Metapsychological Supplement to the Theory of Dreams).

The simple and basic foundation of my theory lies in the fact of the presence in the ego, as is well known in psychoanalysis, of a determined type of psychic energy called *counter-cathexis,* which neutralizes psychic energies on their way to the (pre)-conscious system. Bearing this in mind, let us consider some psychic states in which reality testing is altered, as, for instance, in hallucinatory states that consist simply in believing that what comes from within the psyche is of external origin.

In the first place, I shall examine the traumatic neurosis, a mental disorder that has often served as the starting point for analytic studies. We know that during the trauma which precipitates a traumatic neurosis, a great number of stimuli flood the psyche. In traumatic neurosis, the ego has been unable to mobilize a sufficiently strong counter-cathexis to control and regulate the overwhelming psychic energy produced by the trauma. The sufferer from traumatic neurosis behaves as if he did not perceive the trauma as a memory; instead, in recurrent attacks or dreams he hallucinates the trauma anew, believing that he is actually experiencing it again. The memory of the trauma exists in the unconscious of the traumatized individual, but owing to a deep disturbance of his reality testing, this memory is not perceived consciously as such but appears rather as a repetition of the external traumatic event. This causes him to act repeatedly as if it originated in the outer world, because the particular disturbance of reality testing is a failure on the part of the ego to provide counter-cathexis strong enough to control and elaborate the intense energy of the psychic reactions to the trauma experienced.* In more benign cases, on the days following less intense traumata which are not capable of pro-

* In traumatic neuroses, the different psychical reactions to the trauma, which appear on the days following the trauma, are of internal origin. In other words, the individual does not suffer new external traumata, but he spontaneously continues to react in the way he did to the original trauma, while erroneously perceiving his conduct as induced by some new external trauma. For internal reasons he hallucinates the original exterior trauma again and again.

ducing a traumatic neurosis, the patient remembers the trauma consciously and does not revive it in a hallucinatory fashion. Therefore, since hallucinations are not produced by analogous but less intense traumata, the previously mentioned supposition with regard to the capacity of the counter-cathexis would seem to be logical. The psychic energy which the trauma produces is too powerful for the counter-cathexis of the ego to be able to destroy or control, and therefore it gives rise to hallucinations.

The too intense, internally originated stimuli not being satisfactorily neutralized by an equally strong counter-cathexis, the traumatized patient behaves repeatedly as if he were being subjected again to an external stimulus. The patient is subjected to hallucinations which must be explained by a mechanism contrary to that of Freud's theory regarding reality testing. In the traumatic neurosis the subject erroneously takes for external a traumatic incident which in the first place he was unable to influence by the psychic equivalent of muscular action. According to Freud's theory of reality testing, a danger which one cannot avoid by flight should be perceived as being of intrapsychic origin.

Traumata of variable intensity are followed by repeated hallucinations in dreams, depending upon the subjective state of the victim at the time of the accident. The psychic repetition in the patient during the days following such an experience takes the form either of hallucinatory dreams, when a neurosis ensues, or of simple recollection, when it does not. It is either exogenous or endogenous for the patient, depending on the greater or lesser capacity of his ego to dominate it. This fact has also been clearly stated by Theodor Reik: "Originally, reminiscence implied the attempt to assimilate an experience by reliving it in the imagination. It is, therefore, the repeated performance of a play on the stage of thought or idea, while in the earlier form of action it was really performed again. In the psychopathology of the traumatic neuroses, which so frequently repeat the original situation, the play is performed again, so to speak, because of its overpowering effect."

Bearing this in mind, we can then admit the existence of

a series of analogous psychic phenomena, composed of hallucinations, vivid reproductions in fantasy, and simple recollections. The appearance of one or the other in the patient's psyche depends greatly on the capacity of the ego to dominate an experience by means of counter-cathexis. Forceful counter-cathexis in the ego would be followed by simple recollection; hallucinations would appear if the counter-cathexis were overcome by the stimuli originating in the incident.

If this is so, and if a generalization from the traumatic neuroses is permissible, then all perceptions of internal origin which can be kept within bounds and neutralized in the ego by counter-cathexis are not subjectively considered as originating in external reality. On the contrary, they are considered to proceed from the outer world if they cannot be controlled by counter-cathexis in the ego. If we apply what we have deduced to external perception, we may presume that exogenous sensory perceptions have the characteristics of external reality for the subject because they are more difficult to dominate by counter-cathexis than those which are endopsychic. In other words, external perceptions become (pre)conscious more easily *and with more intensity* than internal perceptions, because the ego is less capable of coping with the former by means of the psychological mechanism of counter-cathexis. It remains to be determined whether this supposition is empirically and theoretically tenable, and what use it may have.

If we examine carefully certain psychic phenomena, we find that the ego more easily rejects things of intrapsychic origin, rather than things which come from without. In fact, all we need do to demonstrate this is to look at the world around us, and then to look within ourselves, at our own personalities. We see a great difference in clarity between one and the other. The things we perceive outside ourselves are clear and precise; those we perceive within ourselves are dark, vague, and undefined. In other words, we have a clear idea of the things around us, but we are unaware of our own personalities, and this is the reason why no one has ever thought to inquire about the shape of things which he sees about him, yet must visit a psychoanalyst to find out about his own character and temperament. It may be stated, psychoanalytically, that the lack of good inner perception is due to a defense mechanism of the ego which rejects, by means of counter-cathexis, ideas and feelings which are inimical to itself. Contrary to what might be supposed, this is not due to the ego's lack of capacity for inner perception. On the contrary, poor perception of external objects or events in certain cases is completely independent of the ego's performance and is solely the result of limitations and imperfections of the senses.

This psychological fact, that external perceptions penetrate the (pre)conscious system with less likelihood of being rejected than inner perceptions, is supported by the observation that the majority of people do not make gross errors (such as hallucinations) in their outer perceptions—yet in intrapsychic perceptions these errors are quite normal. Psychoanalytic treatment enables a person to know himself better, correcting false beliefs he may have entertained about himself, but his perception of the outer world remains more or less the same to him although his affective reaction to it has changed. These examples show that errors in intrapsychic perception do not depend on the ego's lack of capacity to perceive the inner self adequately, but on the effort it makes to reject and modify disagreeable psychic contents. This conduct is impossible when the ego is confronted with facts coming from outer reality, since these have greater resistance to the modifying action of the counter-cathexis.

The fact that the ego rejects inner perceptions rather than outer perceptions explains why psychology has been so late in developing. Until Freud and the present century, a real science of psychology did not exist. As man's prime interest is himself, psychology would have been the first and most perfect of all sciences were it not for the intense rejection of anything psychologically endogenous. This supports my theory that whatever the ego finds easier to reject is perceived as endogenous.

Even with regard to the body, which is closest to the outside world, there is greater rejection of things which originate inside it, so much so that normally the perceptions originating in different organs of the body are not felt consciously despite their undeniable existence, as can be shown by the regulation of organic activity in which superior psychic processes intervene. We must deduce, from the fact that perceptions within the organism are less conscious than those from without, that the ego finds it easier to reject them.

To draw a parallel, it can be said that if perceptions coming from outer reality reached the conscious system with as much difficulty as inner perceptions, we would not consciously perceive the majority of objects or events around us, in exactly the same way as we fail to perceive consciously what is going on within ourselves. This, however, would not destroy the capacity to react adequately to outer reality, for we are able to regulate the functions of our own organism—both mental and physical—pretty well, without being consciously aware of it.

Activity becomes conscious when there is an increase in the intensity of the stimuli from any of the organs, that is, when the ego's counter-cathexis finds rejection more difficult against superior antagonistic forces. This happens, for instance, as a consequence of digestive disturbances, intense muscular activity, or great genital excitation. The relationship of the ego to the outside world is, as we have shown, different, since it easily makes anything that reaches it conscious, the only condition being that it should pass the threshold of excitation of the sensory organs.

A recollection, no matter how vivid and real it may be, is always easier for the ego's counter-cathexis to dominate than a direct sensory perception from the outer world, however weak and indefinite the stimulus may be.* Bearing in mind these easily verifiable facts, we once again state that the ego's reject-

* Outer reality is present in a memory which keeps, to a certain extent, the character of something external because it originated in a perception from the outer world which is not easily dealt with by counter-cathexis. However, memory is not considered external, because it is evoked by internal processes which the ego can dominate with greater facility than external processes.

ing capacity regarding direct external perception must be small, and that reality testing must have as its basis this lesser rejecting capacity.

It is due to this strange behavior of the psyche that hallucinations, whether positive or negative, appear only in extreme pathological cases.* If the ego were able to dominate external perceptions as easily as internal perceptions (as in Freud's theory of reality testing), hallucinatory deformations in perceptions of the outer world would be very common even in normal people.

To take a concrete example: a man does not wish to acknowledge to himself that he is in love with someone. He can repress his affection (which originates internally) more easily than the image (which comes from the external world) of the woman he loves when he sees her; in a situation of rejection he can see her without realizing he loves her. Were the ego equally able to reject the external perceptions, he could maintain his affection and have a negative hallucination: knowing he loves the woman, but not seeing her when she is in front of him. This does not occur because external perceptions are less easily rejected by the ego's counter-cathexis; consequently they act more strongly on the conscious system and therefore impress the ego as coming from the outer world precisely because they could not be rejected or avoided by the ego.

Some objections to this theory are possible. Up to now all my considerations have referred only to a psychic capacity of the ego to reject a perception. As has been proven, this capacity to reject is doubtless less in the case of the perception of some external object than in the case of an intrapsychic one. But, it could be said, Freud's theory does not refer to this point, but to the ego's capacity to reject materially the situation which causes the perception through a voluntary act of separation from the object which provokes it, and this appears to be feasible only with what comes from the external world.

---

* According to Freud, any attempt to explain the psychological problem of hallucination would have to be made from the starting point of a negative hallucination, rather than of a positive one.

Does not this constitute a serious contradiction to the theory here developed?

There is a further objection. According to Freud, among the data which the ego uses to establish the difference between inner and outer perception is the fact that what is internally originated—as, for example, hunger or sadness—is felt for a certain duration of time, no matter how short, while an external discomfort, like a pinprick, is of momentary duration if the ego reacts adequately. Does all this agree with the theory presented here?

Let us examine the objections in detail. The ego can, without doubt, avoid by means of action a painful stimulus of external origin, thereby making it momentary, which does not seem so easily possible with painful endogenous perceptions. Psychoanalysis rightly asserts that one of the ego's faculties is to act upon and modify external reality (alloplasty) to make it more satisfying to the individual's desires. But the problem is not as easy as it appears to be, and this faculty must be examined more closely to see if it exists in all circumstances and, above all, at all ages. To modify external reality is certainly a faculty of the ego, but only of a fully developed ego in possession of an apparatus developed to carry out this modification. Such an apparatus is not developed in infants, when the psychic apparatus is creating and developing the function of reality testing. Alloplasty does not exist in this infantile period; on the contrary, the small child is just as defenseless, or more so, in the face of external reality as it is when confronted by its own internal demands or sensations. Indeed, the infant is unable to modify the discomforts of external reality, such as cold, dampness, or a pinprick, by appropriate muscular activity, nor can it assuage its hunger by getting food for itself. The only thing the child can do in these situations is to react by kicking and crying, which will attract the attention of an adult who can rescue it from its internal or external discomfort. From this we must deduce that the possibility of rejecting outer reality cannot constitute the little child's basis for the genesis of reality testing; yet this important discriminatory function is created and developed in early childhood. Furthermore, if we presume, as seems most probable, that a child has intense perceptions during its birth, this extremely traumatic event would have the effect of favoring to a great extent the development of certain ideas with regard to external reality. This external reality would be regarded as something that acts strongly and continuously on the individual, with the characteristic of being absolutely unavoidable, since it is impossible to avoid the trauma of being born. The deep traces which the intense trauma of birth leaves on the psyche of every individual should be evaluated as an example of the transcendency of this primary situation, when disagreeable, but persistent and inevitable, stimuli are experienced in external reality. We are dealing, then, with an external reality which is quite different from that to be found in Freud's theory of the genesis of reality testing.

Many of the stimuli received by the infant in the course of its early development must have the same effect, although not so intense, as those received during its birth. Theodor Reik calls attention to this when he writes: "Children seem most receptive to new impressions. A French psychologist speaks of the *cerveau de cire* of children and primitive man. This remarkable receptivity may assume the character of the love of sensation. A child is *novum rerum cupidus*. Only a feeble ego confronts this receptivity, and, incapable of mastering so many new impressions, it is forced to hand over the greater part to the unconscious for later assimilation. It is not, therefore, because childish experiences are specially forceful that they are mastered later, but because it is too hard for the feeble ego to master them. In this sense, then, we must attribute a traumatic character not only to particular events but to the sum total of the child's experience." In other words, during infancy, stimuli from the outer world cannot be rejected by the ego, which is forced to submit traumatically to them. The capacity to reject external stimuli cannot, therefore, constitute a positive basis for the formation of reality testing.

From these facts we conclude that at the age when reality

testing is in formation, an examination of the child's possibilities of reacting to the outer world supports the theory that reality testing depends on the ego's lesser capacity for rejecting perceptions of external origin.

This is a further corroboration of my thesis. Nevertheless, let us maintain a critical attitude and declare that my theory should be sustained only if it is able to explain with greater psychological clarity some other important psychic phenomenon, as, for example, the mechanism which operates to produce hallucinations in dreams.

According to Freud's theory, the conditions which permit hallucinations to appear in dreams are regression and defective functioning of the conscious system, the seat of reality testing. But perhaps it is possible to give a more detailed explanation of how the failure of reality testing in dreams occurs. We must suppose that in its desire to maintain sleep, the ego diminishes, although not entirely, the intensity of the counter-cathexis which opposes the free passage to consciousness of rejected id contents, because in order to sleep the ego must also let its energy (of which the counter-cathexis is part) rest. This is a well-known phenomenon in psychoanalysis. The study of dreams clearly shows that forbidden desires, which in a waking state are rejected or repressed, reach consciousness in dreams. In sleep the selective censoring function of the ego is lessened. We have already shown that a certain positive capacity of the ego to reject id contents by means of its counter-cathexis gives rise to the idea that what has been perceived is not of external origin. It is easy to understand, then, that when in sleep the intensity of the ego's counter-cathexis diminishes, those mental contents that were rejected during waking hours (and that, unlike the ego, seem to have no desire to sleep, and therefore maintain their usual energy) will, on finding smaller resistance from the diminished counter-cathexis, act more strongly on the conscious system than in waking hours. Consequently, when these contents reach consciousness as dream activity, the reality testing function of the weakened ego erroneously judges them to be of external origin, precisely because their cathectic charge is relatively greater than the weakened counter-cathexis which is insufficiently mobilized to reject them.

In the previous chapter I developed the theory that hallucinations in dreams arise because the basis of a dream (the compound formed by the day residues and the latent repressed desires) cannot be elaborated normally by the ego, and a traumatic situation is thus created. It would come to be something like a miniature traumatic situation. Similar to a traumatic neurosis, such a situation would be the cause of the aforementioned whole taking on a hallucinatory aspect instead of rising to consciousness as common thoughts. Keeping to this theory of a traumatic situation as the origin of dreams, we can now explain the genesis of dream hallucinations even more precisely. Indeed, as we have already stated, the ego cannot dominate or elaborate all of the day residues and repressed desires normally. This is clearly shown by the fact that they are repressed during waking hours; however, this factor is not in itself sufficient to explain hallucination, since there is no hallucination whatsoever when one is awake. The decrease of the ego's counter-cathexis is the added factor, for it is this energy that maintains repression during waking hours and rejects intrapsychic contents with sufficient intensity to remove their character of external origin as soon as they are perceived by the conscious system. In waking hours the counter-cathexis avoids traumatic situations by repressing disturbing psychic contents. In sleep the situation is different; these contents partly penetrate the conscious psyche, and in this manner the latent trauma become more or less manifest.

The sleeping ego, then, may be compared to a city that is temporarily poorly defended, and that may be easily overrun and destroyed by a hostile army, however small. In other words, sleep destroys the balance between the forces of repression (which decrease) and the repressed forces (which maintain their intensity). The latter are, therefore, sufficiently strong to break into the conscious system, both forcefully and traumatically, in the guise of hallucinations, thus giving rise to dreams. A second psychic function then intervenes, which attenuates the disagreeable tension of traumatic fantasy, transforming the original latent content into the hallucination that appears in the manifest content of the dream.

The well-known custom of pinching or slapping oneself to find out whether an exciting situation is true or only a dream, is effective because the ego is aroused and fortified, thereby reviving the counter-cathexis. In this way the ego accentuates its capacity for reality testing in a given situation. In such an instance the strengthened counter-cathexis of the ego can more easily reject impulses originating from the id, being, moreover, unable to dispel external reality, which despite these maneuvers persists in all its intensity. What can only be dispelled by muscular activity is judged by the ego as proceeding from the outside world; whatever can be dominated by the counter-cathexis is judged by the ego as being of intrapsychic origin, in this case a dream.

To sum up, we can affirm that the ego judges a determined perception as not coming from the outer world (i.e., as being of intrapsychic origin) by the use of its positive capacity to strongly oppose the stimuli of such a perception by counter-cathexis. Whatever the counter-cathexis is unable to dominate in some way is considered by the ego to originate in external reality.

In other words, if a special dynamic equilibrium exists between the libidinal cathexis that brings about a perception, and the counter-cathexis from the ego that does not allow this perception to pass freely (counter-cathexis dominating), the ego regards what is perceived as intrapsychic, and vice versa.

This special equilibrium may vary either way through modifications in either of the two component forces giving rise to variations in reality testing. When the intensity of the ego's counter-cathexis diminishes, a perception is less effectively dispelled and therefore judged to be of external origin, even though it may be an internal perception. This is what happens in dreams.

If, on the contrary, the intensity of a counter-cathexis increases while the cathexis in relation to an object or an event remains unchanged, then what is perceived will lose its character of reality despite its source from the outside world. This happens in the phenomena of depersonalization which, according to Freud, are due to disagreeable unconscious strivings strongly repressed by the ego. A similar constellation probably occurs in the negative hallucinations of psychosis, if, as Freud states, the ego represses external reality to satisfy the id.* A further increase in the intensity of counter-cathexis results in an end to conscious perception, as is usual with visceral sensations.

If stimuli diminish sufficiently in intensity, perception may cease to exist for the ego. Increase in their intensity without commensurate modification of counter-cathexis tends to cause all perception to be reacted to as exogenous, even though it may be endopsychic. The symptoms of traumatic neurosis are given as an example where, due to the very intense stimuli mobilized by a provoking traumatic incident, the patient subsequently hallucinates repetitively the trauma instead of experiencing it subsequently as a memory.

Schematically, and according to the view we have developed, the genesis of some important disturbances of reality testing are represented as follows:

NO PERCEPTION OF EXTERNAL REALITY

Cathexis too weak	No perception.
Counter-cathexis too strong	Negative hallucinations found in psychosis.

---

* No mention is made of the positive hallucinations of psychosis, because their genesis is rather more complicated. Various processes take part in them simultaneously. For example, in the hallucinations of a paranoic with persecution delusion mania, there is the combined action of intense stimuli (homosexual) and intense counter-cathexis, which provokes projection and the change of love into hate.

INTERNAL PERCEPTION CONSIDERED TO BE EXTERNAL IN ORIGIN

Cathexis too intense	Hallucinations of traumatic neurosis.
Counter-cathexis too weak	Dream hallucinations.

Chapter 8

THE DREAM SCREEN AND THE ISAKOWER PHENOMENON

In a number of profound and ingenious papers, Bertram D. Lewin has described what he calls the "dream screen." This is the generally unperceived, white, empty background of the dream. In ordinary dreams the manifest oneiric content appears on the screen. According to Lewin, it represents the mother's breast as a child sees it while nursing, usually flattened because of the child's proximity to it. And thus it represents the unconscious satisfaction of the desire to feed and fall asleep at the mother's breast (and the desire to be consumed by the breast).

Lewin became aware of the existence of the dream screen in a dream related by one of his patients: "I was quite willing to tell you my dream, but as I was lying there, the dream suddenly turned over and disappeared, like a couple of glass tumblers rolling away."

According to Otto Isakower, large masses which approach during dreams represent the breasts; as they come nearer to the eyes they appear to flatten out. In the dream just referred to the opposite happened: as they got further away they became convex. The patient's dream appeared to be projected onto the apparently flattened surface of the breast. In another of this patient's dreams a railing separated her from the landscape. This represented a metallic support worn by her mother, whose breasts had been removed by operation.

By identifying with the breast, the dreamer consumes herself and sinks into the dream screen, which is the flattened view of the breast. The limits of the ego disappear and reappear only in dreams with manifest content where there is a partial awakening. Ample oral satisfaction is contained in blank dreams.

A cartoon by Gluyas Williams [FIGURE 48] may be interpreted as a confirmation of Lewin's conception of the dream screen. In it a mother is telling her dream to her husband and two children, who react by feeling sleepy. The fact that the family is about to have a meal is related to some extent with

FIGURE 48. Gluyas Williams: The Dream

the psychological situation created by the mother in telling her dream, because the cartoon would not be so funny if the family were doing something different. By following Lewin's theory we can deduce that there is an analogy between the two situations represented in the drawing, i.e., eating and telling the dream. We can also suppose that in telling her dream, the mother, instead of letting her family find satisfaction by eating the food on the table, is leading them toward a similar type of satisfaction, that of feeding at the maternal breast.

There are several details in the drawing that may be viewed from this angle. In the first place, the meal to be eaten is breakfast, in which more milk (or its substitutes, tea or coffee) is drunk than at other meals, and this is shown on the table. The maid, a maternal substitute, is offering the family food that is shaped like a breast, and this could be the reason for the family's feeling sleepy—they have been satisfied at the maternal breast. (If we carry this interpretation even further, we might say that the tray which the maid is carrying represents the flattened view of the maternal breast.) The possibility of satisfying the desire to feed at the mother's breast is shown by the mother being a fat person with large breasts, while the rest of the family appears underfed. The cartoon's caption confirms these interpretations to a certain extent, because it describes the mother's dream, which in the beginning is about food.

If these interpretations are correct, the artist's inclusion of a picture on the wall entitled "Le Rêve" is his unconscious indication that falling asleep at the mother's breast plays its part in the genesis of dreams. It depicts a sylvan setting, in which an ample nude woman is asleep in a recumbent position with an angel hovering over her.

Lewin's original observations have been amply corroborated by many psychoanalysts who have reported dreams confirming his conclusions. For example, a patient reported to Dr. Lawrence S. Kubie, "the worst nightmare of his childhood . . . an endless wall . . . like . . . a milky substance," which represented the flattened breast of the mother as it appears in the dream screen.

Lewin and Kubie report that very often these dreams cause anxiety, and in the dream the dreamer resorts to manic defenses to escape from threatening dangers. The dreamer has "immeasurable superiority to the danger from which he is fleeing." The cause of anxiety in these dreams is the representation of the mother's breast. The dreamer flees from it with the help of his mother's "immeasurable superiority," since he must undoubtedly remember how, after his mother had fed him as a baby, she removed him from the breast with movements that must have seemed enormous to him, in view of his size. In later years these movements that separate him from the terrifying breast appear in dreams as enormous liberating leaps.

According to Lewin, in this dream and other similar dreams the "whitish, cloudy, endless wall is the breast or ghost of a breast." "Ghost of a breast" suggests that besides referring to the parents' night clothes, as pointed out by Freud, the white sheet with which ghosts are depicted in comic drawings is also a representation of the dream screen. This is reflected in the habit of many infants of sleeping with their sheets or pillows pressed over their mouths.

The presence of something that represents the flattened view of the breast, and thus covers some of the manifest content of the dream (in the same way as the white sheet covers the ghost in funny drawings), can occasionally be shown when dreams are analyzed. For example, the following dream:

133] *A doctor, X, offers me a white Chesterfield cigarette. The dream had a sort of white background.*

As he told me of his dream, the patient mentioned the whiteness of the cigarette. The dream was a reaction by the patient to an interpretation of mine which had helped to improve his financial situation. The white background visible in the dream is quite clearly the dream screen as described by Lewin. The white covering of the cigarette, which the patient commented on, is somewhat similar. His associations clearly showed that both represented the breast. For example, the Dr. X of the dream, who represents the analyst, is always inviting the patient to have coffee with him, and always urges the patient to ask his wife to feed him cream so that he will put on weight. In other words, the doctor who gives him the *white* cigarette symbolizes the mother who feeds him milk from her breast.

A deeper meaning in the dream is a protest against the analyst, who, although he has calmed the patient's desire to be fed by favorably resolving his economic difficulties, has not yet been able to improve the patient's genital potency. With regard to this the patient associated that Chesterfield cigarettes are shorter than Pall Malls, which he prefers; a Pall Mall means for him a longer and more potent penis than his own.

The patient continued with associations referring to adequate alimentary and deficient genital satisfaction, and ended by reporting that the previous day his wife had given him a good meal, but she had forgotten to give him any fruit for dessert. This could be interpreted that after eating she had not offered to have intercourse with him, and that this was her usual mode of behavior.

The interpretation of the parts of the dream that related to the dream screen—the white of the cigarette and the breast—were not communicated to the patient. Because of this, he had further associations of the same type the following day. He said he had read a book on psychoanalysis, and he associated the *two white pages* of the open book with two breasts (flattened); cigarette ash which was lying between the pages, "in the cleft of the book," he thought of as excrement, semen, and bad mother's milk, which he called excrement. He then spoke of a female psychoanalyst, whom he considered pretty but frustrating, and he represented her as having her breasts full of worms, which looked like excrement, i.e., full of bad, anal milk. He then spoke of another woman who had *flattened breasts*, as if a pane of glass had been laid over them. He associated his mother and her nourishing breasts with this woman. All these associations help confirm that the white paper of the cigarette in the dream symbolized for the patient a flattened breast from which to feed.

Months later, when another of his dreams was being analyzed, the same association emerged, referring this time to the *white* armbands worn by a traffic policeman.

This patient had undergone intense regression to an oral-digestive stage. He lived with his wife as though she were his mother, practically without sexual relations and frequently depending on her family for financial support. He denied the existence of genitality in himself and in his wife, and his unconscious fantasies about his wife's being unfaithful to him took on the conscious aspect that his wife might be attacked in the street. A burglary at a shop nearby increased these unconscious fears. That same night, while waiting for his wife to come home, he felt very uneasy. He lay down, not in the usual way but across the bed, with his mouth pressed against the sheet. Lying like this, he kicked the bed like a hungry child calling for its mother. In this state of mind he fell asleep and had a dream:

134] *A Mr. Wolf, whom I do not know, was sitting at the table with other people.*

A streetcar which passed by half awoke him from this dream, and he then perceived that:

My dream was becoming flattened, turning into something like a photograph and then disappearing upwards, like a curtain. Only a white, milky background remained, rather like a television screen.

The unknown Mr. Wolf, who was at table with other people, symbolized a possible rival in bed with his wife, expressed in oral-digestive terms. The sound of the streetcar reminded him of the shots fired during the burglary at the shop. It also made him think that his wife was about to arrive, because she always came home by streetcar.

During his psychoanalytic session he went on to say that there was a traffic policeman on the corner near his home, where the streetcar passed. He emphasized the policeman's two white armbands in the same way as the whiteness of the cigarette in the previous dream. He thereupon remarked that this policeman might have prevented the burglary at the shop, just as he would have stopped the patient's wife from showing her naked breasts to other men living near their flat. The armbands symbolized his wife's breasts, which the policeman (analyst) looked after so that they should continue to belong to the patient. The sound of the streetcar calmed him by suggesting his wife's arrival. It therefore eliminated from his dream the disturbing symbol of marital infidelity, which was Mr. Wolf. There remained in the dream only the image symbolizing satisfaction at the mother's breast—the white, milky background of the dream which represented a television screen.

The anxiety that had been stimulated by the introduction of Mr. Wolf into the dream disappeared when the sound of the streetcar led to oral regression through a mechanism which Lewin has pointed out with regard to the forgetting of dreams. This regression made the dream become flat and turn into something like a curtain, an image of the flattened maternal breast, which finally disappeared from the field of perception.

In the dream reported to Kubie that we have already mentioned, "a whitish wall" represented the flattened breast. An analogous dream, with a wall as the breast, but in which the morphological characteristics of the breast may be better observed, was related to I. P. Glauber, and I reproduce it here in order to compare it later with one of my own patients' dreams:

135] *It was a wall pinkish in color. The patient called it a "screen" which was set up between him and the analyst. The wall was punctuated by elevations, which on closer view turned out to be roses, which he associated with the areola around the nipple. The center of the rose, he elaborated, had an elevation which he associated with the penis, and he described the erectile qualities of the center.*

As Lewin has pointed out, dreams of this type come from

infantile fantasies, plus those which occur during the first months of breast feeding, and in them we find more precise representations of the maternal breast.

Such representations of the breast lead the child to associate the erectile nipple with the penis, as we see in the dream contributed by Glauber. According to Lewin, when a child is able to stand on its own feet, the image of the flat abdominal wall is added to its earlier representation of a flattened breast. This permits fantasies of sleeping in the womb to be superimposed upon those of sleeping upon or within the breast.

One of my patients had a dream like that of Kubie's patient, and even more like that of Glauber's; it was about a wall which represented the flattened breast, but which also functioned as a screen that reflected objects.

136] *On a palisade of bricks I saw reflected a white meteor, which was about to fall and blow up the earth.*

The palisade symbolized the flat breast, and the pink elevations of the bricks represented the areola and the nipples.

The patient's term "palisade of bricks" seemed inappropriate, because a palisade is made of wood. This mistake was not analyzed, but the latent content of the dream suggests that the sticks of the palisade symbolized the penis and also the teeth of the child seeking oral satisfaction at the breast.

Glauber's patient dreamed of a wall like a "screen" between him and the analyst. In my patient's dream, the wall that represents the flattened breast, as seen by the suckling child, clearly acts as a reflecting screen, for it reflects a white meteor. This meteor by its form and color also represents the breast, but this breast is not flat. In this dream, therefore, the wall that is the dream screen, the flattened breast, reflects the meteor which is the rounded breast as seen by the child when he is further away from it.

My patient associated the meteor in her dream with pregnancy and a penis containing white semen (in Spanish, semen is commonly called "milk"). At the time of the dream, the patient was worrying about being pregnant. With the exploding of the meteor she associated abortion and childbirth, also the scandal that would burst when her pregnancy became known. She was in a great state of anxiety because of her strong dependence on her family.

During her childhood, when the patient stopped sleeping in her parents' room, she repeatedly had unpleasant sensations in her throat, rather as though she had bubbles in it. She also had the impression that the whole of the floor in her new room was padded.

The bubbles represented her mother's breasts, and because she had been removed from her parents' room, these stuck in her throat. It was also deduced from her associations that, by its resemblance to the mattress of her parents' bed, the padded floor of her room represented the breast, but flattened as when seen from too close. In this impression of the padded floor, the scene oscillated between impressions of the breast as seen close and from a distance (as in the patient's previous dream of the wall and the meteor), because, as the patient said, a mattress or anything which is upholstered is flat, but it has rounded corners and buttons; to her these symbolized breasts and nipples.

The day following this analysis, because of her intense anxiety, this patient once again had the uncomfortable feeling of bubbles in her throat, for the first time in many years. Besides its childhood meaning of breasts, this sensation now meant testicles and pregnancy, which disagreed with her. That morning she had paid an unusual amount of attention to her underclothes, particularly her brassiere, for she now felt it did not become her. She thought her breasts were fuller. This was also a representation of pregnancy. All this confirms the fact that the white meteor in her previous dream signified the breast.

She next associated frigidity with the wall in her dream. As in Glauber's case, the wall was something that separated her from other people. She added that the wall corresponded to all the front parts of a woman's body, from the genitals to the neck, and, as she insisted, the "passage between the breasts."

In all these associations there is an oscillation between fantasies of the breast and others of the mother's belly. The fantasies are intermediate, as Lewin points out, between those of a child being given the breast—and who sees the breast as flat, and those of a somewhat older child who, because it can stand up, sees the mother's belly rather than her breast.

In this dream there is a double representation of the breast, which appears both as a wall, which acts as a screen, and as a white meteor. This corresponds to the child's different views of the breast—flat when he is feeding at it, round when he moves away from it.

This double representation is probably very common, for it is also frequently found in folklore customs. In some regions of Mexico, when there is an eclipse of the moon, the Indians sing songs while looking at the moon reflected in vessels full of water. These vessels probably symbolize the gratifying maternal breast. The double image of the moon, first direct, then again reflected in the water, has caused intense emotion in human beings, as is shown by the existence of many paintings and poems on the subject.

Because it shows this unconscious situation, a drawing of Peter Arno's makes us laugh. The drawing shows a man in a boat, with an expression on his mouth and in his eyes that denotes intense instinctual satisfaction. His nose is long, like an erect penis. He makes his companion row so that he can see her large breasts every time she leans forward. The moon is reflected in the water, symbolizing the gratifying maternal breast. Had the setting been different, the cartoon would not have been so funny, although it would have been easier for the man to see the girl's breasts in daylight. Lewin has pointed out that in this cartoon the mountains in the background look like teeth about to bite the moon.

Lewin has also described blank dreams which represent the "complete fulfillment of the wish to sleep at the mother's breast after nursing." These blank dreams have no visual content, but their presence can be demonstrated, for example, when the dreamer has an orgasm in his sleep.

Lewin observed these dreams in the case of a schizophrenic patient with a strong mother fixation. On four occasions, after ample oral satisfaction with a mother substitute, the patient said she had a dreamless sleep, but orgasms occurred. These blank sexual dreams usually came before hypomanic states; during them the patient suffered from heterosexual delusions in which she realized the contents that had been absent from the dreams. The dream was a repetition of the childhood situation of having just been fed at the breast; it referred only to the breast and satisfied the desire to sleep. It was a primary dream in which the ego played no part and produced no conflicts. Dreams with manifest contents come from other desires, not that of sleeping.

In these dreams the invisible dream screen would be the representation of the breast which satisfies completely, while in ordinary dreams "the visual elements represent psychic elements which interfere with the desire to sleep." In other words, as Lewin says, unsatisfied desires are the cause of the visible content of dreams.

Lewin's affirmations regarding oral and genital aspects are amply confirmed by the dream I have just studied—the "white cigarette on a white background." The psychoanalyst was able to improve the patient's financial situation and thus give him intense oral-digestive satisfaction; had this been all, it doubtless would have given rise to a blank dream with perhaps an orgasm. But the patient had further aspirations, so his oral-digestive satisfaction was not complete. These not totally satisfied alimentary aspirations gave rise to a dream with the visible dream screen as the white background. Added to this was the fact that economic improvement did not improve the patient's genital potency, the main achievement he had hoped to draw from his psychoanalytic treatment. Therefore, on the visible white background of the dream, there appeared the manifest content of the cigarette, which was a phallic symbol. The patient thus expressed dissatisfaction with his genital potency by choosing a cigarette that was too short.

A patient reported to Charles Rycroft a dream with a white

background which he compared to a sheet. The latent dream thoughts resembled those in my patient's dream; they expressed the patient's feeling that he was protected by his analyst, and also his longing for greater oral and genital satisfaction from him. According to Rycroft, the dream screen appears in psychoanalytic treatment when the patient abandons a position of narcissistic identification and dares to seek satisfaction in objects, even if he does so with anxiety.

The sources of the various kinds of dreams—ordinary dreams with visible contents, blank dreams, and nearly blank dreams—are various situations in which satisfaction is or is not attained. These sources are often masked, for the sleeper wishes to free himself from traumatic unconscious situations of dissatisfaction and would rather pay attention to those that produce complete satisfaction. This is one reason why the sleeper may strive to sleep without dreams. Sometimes he succeeds in avoiding awareness of the manifest aspect of the dream, but the concomitant affectivity is much more difficult to mask. His blank dreams awaken him as though they were terrifying nightmares. As Lewin points out, they thus seem to nullify their own function, which is to express satisfaction of the wish to feed and sleep at the breast. This occurs because the apparent wish fulfillment which forms the content of blank dreams does not allay the anxiety and soothe the latent traumata, but rather reinforces them. Thus blank dreams, with or without anxiety, may occur during the same night as dreams with visible contents, all arising from a single latent situation of trauma or lack of satisfaction.

This happened to one of my patients. He had gone to sleep in a state of anxiety the night before and had had a nightmare "like those I had when I was small." At first he said that the nightmare was entirely without content. Then, without noticing that he was contradicting himself, he went on to say that he had dreamed of:

137] A *contraceptive sheath filled with water.*

The day residue of the visible content of his dream was that the night before he had washed a sheath he had used.

The patient, whose surroundings were unhappy, had suffered from frequent nightmares during his childhood; he would awake from these in a state of anxiety and call for his mother. These nightmares either had no visible content or were very vague—"something like clouds or circles which became larger or smaller." They were, therefore, blank or nearly blank dreams. When he grew up he had similar nightmares after having been frustrated in achieving satisfaction during the day.

On the day he reported the dream, he came to his psychoanalytic session in a state of "floating anxiety, with no precise content" (a description reminiscent of blank dreams), caused by the fact that he was going to have to read a paper in public, a prospect that caused him both anxiety and pleasure. The day before he had had sexual intercourse which had given him little pleasure because of the use of a condom. After intercourse he had dozed on the woman's breast, and he must have suffered anxiety because she told him that he had been twitching in his sleep. It was later that night when he had the nightmare like he had when a boy.

When his nightmare was analyzed, it appeared that the sheath full of water symbolized for him the maternal breast full of milk, but the breast was not for him, in the same way as, during the day, he had not enjoyed intercourse. He had not been able to throw away the condom, and he associated this with the fact that he had few libidinous objects, and because of this felt the need to hoard the ones he had; that in childhood he had had few satisfactions from his mother and family, who nevertheless tried to convince him that he was a pampered child.

The latent oral-digestive component in all this was made evident by the patient. He said, for instance, that in deceiving him with false endearments, his relatives had made him "take holy communion with windmills" (an expression which in Spanish means "to deceive"), and he spoke of the harmful things which his mother had made him *swallow* which gave him heartburn, and a feeling that his mother had poisoned him. The night of the unsatisfactory coitus and the nightmare, he took a drink to help him go to sleep, a further sign of his lack of oral-digestive satisfaction, which he sought to compensate by having a drink and sleeping.

To sum up, this patient's blank or nearly blank dreams in childhood were due to his intense lack of instinctual satisfaction, which he tried to disguise by having this type of wish-fulfilling dream.

There was a predominance of oral elements, either original or regressive, in his infantile lack of satisfaction. When he grew up, he again had this type of dream, which acted as a dream screen onto which he projected other dreams with very visible contents, and these appeared when he experienced situations with a lack of genital satisfaction, which, through regressive processes, turned into a lack of oral-digestive satisfaction, such as he had suffered in infancy.

This patient's childhood nightmares were of clouds and circles of various sizes, and constituted what Lewin calls the "Isakower phenomenon," as it was Isakower who first described it. The phenomenon occurs in hypnagogic hallucinations and dreams and consists of images of limitless, whitish, amorphous masses or discs that may revolve or grow larger or smaller, may hum, come near, go away, or envelop the sleeper, and may also produce sensations in his mouth.

All these impressions and sensations are derived from those of the young child who sleeps at the mother's breast and has fantasies of having this breast all around it and in its mouth, or of being itself within the breast. According to Lewin, the dream screen is a form of the Isakower phenomenon.

This would appear to be confirmed in a graphic way in the representation of dreams in comic strips, where they appear in the middle of a cloud. This cloud functions as the dream screen, since the subject of the dream is projected onto it. (Also in comic strips a similar cloud appears as a "balloon" enclosing the speech of the persons portrayed. This constitutes a stylization of the representation and corresponds to the concreteness of oneiric images passing into the abstraction of speech.)

The visible Isakower phenomenon in dreams, hypnagogic hallucinations, or nightmares results from a latent frustration or traumatic situations. This is shown by the example just cited and by Gert Heilbrunn's analysis of his own recurrent nightmare of a huge, amorphous mass that approached him, roaring ominously. It first occurred when he was three years old. He connected it with two screen memories of that time, memories of satisfaction and frustration, one of staying at the home of a woman with large breasts, the other a realization that other people were eating raspberries and leaving him none. It was a memory of oral-digestive and genital frustrations.

These examples show that childhood oral-digestive frustrations can unite with later impressions to produce either the Isakower phenomenon or the visible dream screen.

Another example of the Isakower phenomenon, with both oral-digestive and genital determinants, was reported by a patient who in his childhood had had a nightmare with the following content:

138] *A circle was revolving at great speed and getting smaller while at the same time making a buzzing noise.*

The anxiety that caused the revolving circle was the result of several traumatic experiences in childhood. The patient grew up with an aunt who took great interest in him until she acquired a lover. The audibly revolving circle symbolized his aunt's intercourse with her lover, which he used to hear, and the threatening words with which his aunt warned him to tell no one what was happening. It also represented other threatening words his aunt used when she discovered him masturbating, and the noise he made when he masturbated. The receding circle symbolized his mother's breast, which instead of satisfying him in early childhood, as it should have done, receded from him. He was not nursed by his mother, and he watched with envy while she nursed his younger brothers; he again felt intense envy when his own children were suckled by his wife. When these childhood memories became conscious during psychoanalysis, important changes took place in the patient. He felt as though a fog that was constantly in his head (similar to the Isakower phenomenon) was clearing up. At the same time, his intense dislike for a woman he knew grew less. The patient had heard that this woman had often had intercourse with her lover instead of preparing supper for her younger brother with whom she lived. The situation resembled that of his own childhood, with the addition of the lack of food—important for him because he had lacked his mother's milk. Later he was able to remember his aunt not as the old woman she now was but as she had been, a woman of youth and beauty, of whom he had long repressed conscious memories.

These phenomena appear not only in dreams but in other manifestations of human fantasies, such as poetic descriptions: "Tonight I have followed a man; long have I walked behind his shadow, with no other scene but the swinging of his thin shoulders under the opaque blue cloth . . . I have the feeling of having pursued him always.

"My pursuit has been implacable since I discovered . . . the monotony of a blue landscape, pathless, rainless . . . I would weep if this blue wall that parts me from all things should fade into a street opening . . . I have pursued him all through life . . . My eyes now gaze from that limited and moving welkin of his body . . . I have the feeling of having passed through his body and being no longer pursuer but pursued. . . .

"Thus we walked, almost fused together, like strange lovers, for a timeless space . . . My feet glide noiselessly, adhering to his shadow, along the brilliant pavement, upon which his silhouette lengthens and shortens, alternately, forever. Suddenly, a mouth of light swallows him . . . Once more I am confronted with myself, confronted with my misery."

The author of these lines underwent analysis by Marcela Spira. The story derived from a "wish to be fused to her mother through her mouth, i.e., fused to her mother's breast." The oral-digestive nature of the story is also shown by such expressions as "fade into a street opening" (in Spanish, the expression is literally "street mouth"), and "to be swallowed by a mouth of light." In the story there are many symbols of the breast seen as flat, for example, the blue wall or cloth; as spherical, in the shoulders; and of the Isakower type, as in the shadow through which the protagonist passes. An inverted screen can be seen in the detail of the shadow that is reflected on the brilliant pavement. The blue color of the wall or cloth results from a projection of the image of the breast onto the sky as representative of the encompassing world, a projection that is followed by a return to the breast, as shown by the reference to the eyes which "now gaze from that limited . . . welkin of his body"; this return makes these symbols of the breast blue.

Chapter 9

DEVIATIONS FROM PSYCHOANALYTIC INTERPRETATION

Current scientific literature on the interpretation of dreams is completely under psychoanalytic influence, but there are authors whose conclusions differ to a greater or lesser degree from those of psychoanalysis. The only important modifications to the psychoanalytic theory of dreams have been made by Stekel, Jung, and Adler, founders of psychological schools with special ideas.

The nearest to Freud is Wilhelm Stekel, who has written various books worth reading. Outstanding among these is *The Language of Dreams*, in which he gives accurate and clear-sighted interpretations of dreams. In addition to expounding Freud's ideas, he describes new dream symbols which he discovered with a great deal of psychological insight. They are, for instance, the symbol of right to left, of the examination dream, and of others concerning death. But Stekel suffers from insufficient critical evaluation and has an exaggerated tendency toward generalization, which makes it advisable that he be read with considerable caution.

Stekel has introduced a modification of psychoanalysis, which he calls "active analysis," and with which he claims to shorten the treatment. It consists of interpreting dreams independently from the patient's associations. According to him, the analyst must feel, with intuition and experience, what happens in the patient's psyche without using associations, or, at least, by making less use of them, as they only prolong treatment. To achieve this he uses the method of "simplification." This means reducing the dream to a brief sketch, a few words that represent the essential plot of the dream.

While remaining true to his original ideas of dream interpretation, Stekel has introduced some changes, explained first in *The Dream of Poets* and later in *The Interpretation of Dreams*, a collection of his papers of different periods. The analysis of some chapters of the latter book will give a fair view of Stekel's dream psychology, by showing how he largely follows the standards set by Freud.

In "Representation of Parapathetic Symptoms in Dreams," published in 1907, he cited various dreams in which the neurosis is symbolized by people. Thus the first dream of a patient during psychoanalysis was as follows:

139] *King Alfonso of Spain is informed that an attempt is to be made on his life.*

This patient was born on the same day as the King of Spain and therefore identified with him. In the dream the King was the symbol of the neurosis which dominated him, and which the psychoanalytic treatment was trying to destroy, i.e., making an attempt on his life.

Another similar dream:

140] *My girl friend has decided to leave me. I implore her to stay with me, but she refuses."You know that Dr. Stekel can't stand me . . ."*

A patient had the following dream a few days before giving up treatment:

141] *Lily, a servant who has been with us for twenty years, is dying. Dr. Stekel is leaning over her bed and listening* *to her heart with a stethoscope. "It will soon be over," he tells me. "Oh, no!" I reply, "she will go on living for a long time."*

The neurosis that will reappear after the end of treatment is represented by the servant.

Stekel cites the different symbols which may represent neurosis in dreams. This series of observations was completed in 1935 in another paper on "Representation of Neurotic Symptoms in Dreams," referring not to neurosis in general but to particular aspects of it. In this paper he studies asthma, stammering, erythrophobia, trigeminus neuralgia, epilepsy, impotence, frigidity, leucorrhea, dysmenorrhea, homosexuality, fetishism, masochism, and schizophrenia.

Thus, in the case of stammering, the dreams express a difficulty in speaking.

142] *I had to climb a mountain. There were many obstacles. I had to jump a ditch, or climb over a hedge, and then stop because I was out of breath.*

In stammering there are two kinds of symbols: those which represent repressed impulses and those which point out the impediment of speech.

The following are dreams of erythrophobics:

143] *I stand on the shore of a lake where the water is quite calm. Suddenly a storm arises so that waves break on the shore and my face is splashed.*

I see an island in the sea, and it looks sinister. Dark clouds suddenly gather, and the island is covered with fog.

In other dreams, blushing appears as dirtying the face, as passing through dirty places, undressing, or discovering hidden sinful thoughts.

Trigeminal neuralgia:

144] *I am driving a streetcar. A baby carriage blocks the way. By shoving it aside I can go on. As I drive there are* *always three horses in front of me. One of them continually tries to bite me and this interferes with my driving.*

The patient wishes to lead his own life but is hindered by his infantilism—the baby carriage—and by the pain in one of the three branches of the trigeminal nerve, symbolized by the horses.

The content of falling appears in epileptics' dreams.

145] *I am climbing higher and higher up a ladder. Suddenly I notice that several rungs are missing, and my foot gropes vainly for support.*

In a cyclopathic patient, the recurrence of the illness and his mental disturbance are symbolized in the dream:

146] *I see a glass cylinder in which a herring swims round and round, always in the same direction. Gradually the fluid becomes clouded, milky, and this alarms me very much.*

Another chapter refers to the patient's relationship to his analysis as expressed in his dreams. Dreams express the patient's past and his reaction to treatment. Not keeping this last point in mind may cause therapy to fail.

Among other examples, Stekel analyzes again the dream of a patient whose clinical history was published by Sadger:

147] *A room in which there are other persons besides myself. An old woman, whose days seem to be numbered, goes into an adjoining room, and all those present bid her a cordial farewell. I am the last to do so and try to say something most encouraging while wishing her better health. She smiles an indescribable, weary smile. I see my mother with her eyes full of tears and feel extremely sorry for her. My compassion made me promise to marry her. When she looked less distressed and I was no longer so full of pity, I regretted a little my promise of marriage; I was afraid that since she was so fickle, we would not be particularly happy together.*

Sadger interprets this dream as indicating the transfer of love from the grandmother to the mother, after the grandmother's death. This is possible, but Stekel, on the basis of the patient's associations, points out that the grandmother also personifies Dr. Sadger, who, according to the patient, never treated him well; hence his reason for abandoning the treatment, as other patients, represented by the other persons at the beginning of the dream, had also done. The mother symbolizes the neurosis itself, from which the patient will continue to suffer because of the failure of therapy.

In *Dreams and Intuition* Stekel asserts that dreams are overdetermined, but that their essential constituent is the attempt to find a solution to the dreamer's most important conflictual problems. Sometimes the psychoanalyst reaches an intuitive solution which clears up this determining factor. This does not mean that the psychoanalyst should do without the patient's associations, but that, as these deviate from the main conflict, a true intuitive interpretation is necessary.

Among the examples cited by Stekel, there is one of a young man of a very religious family who married a dancer and led a very unhappy married life. This can be seen in a dream:

148] *I am walking along a narrow path between a stormy sea on the left and an abyss on the right. Occasionally there is a flash of lightning. In front of me walks a little boy carrying a lantern; following the light I reach a lighthouse and know that I am saved.*

The storm symbolizes the young man's mental disturbance and the fact that he cannot solve his conflicts by changing his way of life. The flashes of lightning are fleeting moments of clarity in his mind. The boy is Jesus, and the lighthouse the church to which the repentant dreamer wishes to return.

In another case a woman, who has had a secret affair with a man from Munich for over a year, is thinking of a possible marriage of convenience.

149] *I want to go to Munich by train and am at the ticket* *window to get my ticket. As I open my purse, I am surprised that instead of the hundred-shilling note I thought I had, there is only an old postage stamp, torn at one corner. However, I hand it to the clerk, who has now changed into an employee of the art museum, whose task is to clean and restore old paintings. To my amazement he accepts my stamp, hands over my ticket to Munich with the change from a hundred shillings, and I go on to the platform. Many passengers are looking out of the windows. Although my luggage has already been placed in my compartment, I call for someone as if my luggage had still to be put into the car.*

The old and wrinkled stamp is the dreamer's hymen, already torn. She deceives the ticket seller with the stamp, and later all the people, by making believe that her luggage is still outside the train, i.e., that she has not had sexual relations before. The restorer of pictures arises from the idea of having her hymen restored.

Irreparable losses of parts of the body often represent the loss of the hymen, and among Jews, the loss of the prepuce. The latter is the case of a man who wanted a job for which it was necessary to be a Christian:

150] *In early childhood I had lost an eyelid. I go to a surgeon to see whether it can be replaced. He says that no such operation has yet been invented. I tell him that this defect is a hindrance to my career.*

In another case a young woman dreamed that she had lost a big toe. With the dream she recalled her defloration by her brother when she was sixteen.

In a dream referring to the bible, when the patient mentioned only the words "Holy Scriptures" without speaking of the Old and New Testaments, the expression led Stekel to discover intuitively that he referred to a second will the father had made in favor of the patient. The same thing happened in another dream in which the dreamer spoke to a woman who said she was his wife but was not, and who had a rough and disagreeable voice. From this last detail it was possible to deduce that this referred to a sister to whom the patient was genitally fixated, in other words, who had been his "wife" since childhood.

The dream of an impotent journalist:

151] *I see half a horse lying on the ground. It has only one wing; it wants to get up but cannot.*

He was a man whose marriage had forced him to abandon his literary ambitions. Stekel discovered that the horse in the dream was Pegasus mutilated in the struggle for existence. The patient confirmed the interpretation and pointed out in addition that his wife called his penis "Pegasus," and that when he was impotent she would say that Pegasus had lost his wings.

Stekel describes the case of a woman with very intense attacks of vomiting and anxiety. Her husband suffered from premature ejaculation, so that she never had an orgasm. One of her last dreams during psychoanalysis was as follows:

152] *In 1690 Empress Maria Theresa lost her son. Today it is a hundred years since he died.*

The incongruity of the dream is explained by examining the latent material. The Empress Maria Theresa of Austria represents the mother-in-law who, like the patient, had many children. The lost son is the patient's husband who has died as a love object. They had been married seven years (1 plus 6); 9 refers to the years of intimacy and also to the months of pregnancy; 0 to the lack of orgasm. The end of the dream can be understood by realizing that the woman's marriage seems eternal to her, or at least as long as a century.

The patient had an intense fixation on her father, which after her marriage was displaced onto her father-in-law; this appears in the following dream with a very clear genital content:

153] *I am in the kitchen. It is dark. My father-in-law comes* *in to fetch some water; he stumbles and falls over me onto the floor, so that he is lying on top of me.*

In another dream, also easy to understand, her conflicts between genitality and religion appear. Intercourse is symbolized by the drinking of beer and the number 4 refers to a love affair she was told about:

154] *I am in church, near the high altar, and I serve four glasses of beer. I am surprised that people drink beer in church. There is confusion, noise, and bustle. Someone approaches me from behind and takes a glass of beer out of my hand. I feel that I am behaving wrongly.*

A melancholy girl, whose fiancé suffered castration as a result of an accident, dreamed:

155] *I am wearing a torn dress, open from right to left. My sister's dress is also torn, but not open.*

A letter from my fiancé, which contains some verses. Then he is there in person. He says, "Your brother lacks energy." It concerns something which someone has to do.

Stekel quickly interprets the first part as a confession of lost virginity and the second part as the opposite meaning—the brother had too much energy and had had sexual relations with his sister. This was then confirmed by the patient as having happened when she was ten years old. She had kept it secret, but it had already appeared in a previous dream:

156] *I had received a letter from one of my friends. I opened it but did not read it. There was a wide black border around the envelope, and on it a pink rose, or rather a rose bud, was embossed.*

The bud is virginity, and the rose a woman with sexual experience. An open or closed letter repeats this meaning. Not to read the letter is to deny what happened. The black border is her unhappiness about her defloration.

In a *Case of Dyspareunia*, Stekel refers to a married woman who was frigid in her marriage but showed great orgiastic capacity with a vulgar lover whom she despised. The analysis of a dream helped to uncover the latent trauma which dated from puberty. When she was a young girl she had fallen in love with the pastor of her church, and she had been greatly disappointed when he married a woman far beneath him. Psychoanalysis resolved this repressed conflict, and she subsequently led a happy married life.

In *Dreams of a Homosexual Man,* Stekel describes the treatment of a pervert. He had experienced an important traumatic situation during puberty, when he attempted intercourse with his thirteen-year-old sister, and again the next day with his six-year-old sister who screamed with pain. His remorse was intense; he promised the Virgin never to touch a woman again, thus giving rise to his homosexuality. It was based on an intense fixation on the older sister; all the images of his fantasy, men and women alike, were substitutes for her. Moreover, he had a very significant symptom: he would cut out silhouettes of beautiful women's figures seen from behind and replace their heads with those of men. Stekel interpreted this as a representation of the wish not to see the woman, i.e., the sister.

Treatment lasted three months and was successful. The trauma concerning the sister was discovered only at the end, but its influence was observed in dreams.

Stekel's own methods regarding dreams are described in the chapter referring to "The Technique of Dream Interpretation." He advises such practices as having the patient write down his dreams every day. He insists on the need not to rely exclusively on associations for interpretations, but rather to allow oneself to be led by intuition.

To illustrate dream interpretation, Stekel refers to a case treated by a pupil, with the account of one of his dreams. He explains how to:

1. Simplify the dream.
2. Reduce it to its basic affect.
3. Find its antithesis.

4. Look for the stereotyped elements in a series of dreams.
5. Make a functional interpretation in addition to the interpretation of the material.
6. Find its relationship to illness.
7. Explore its relationship to birth and death.
8. And also to religion.
9. Observe the three main time trends in the dream: the present, the retrospective, and the prospective.
10. Investigate its relationship to homosexuality, heterosexuality, and infantilism, i.e., the trisexual structure of the dream.
11. Study the anagogic and catagogic trends.
12. Observe how the dream discloses the patient's dominant idea.

Silberer's so-called functional interpretation considers the content of the dream as a representation of the thought process; it often coincides with what Jung calls "interpretation upon the subjective stage." To explain both functional and material interpretations, Stekel cites this dream:

157] *Barefoot, with my trousers rolled up above the knees, I cross the cold snow with the ladder that leads into the loft. I hasten past my father, who looks at me severely and gloomily, and knock at the door above. The door is locked. My mother opens it; she gives me shoes and stockings and says, "You can come whenever you like. I shall always be here waiting for you."*

From the functional point of view, the dream represents the voice of conscience. The father looks at the man with anger, but the mother, the Virgin Mary, pardons him and is always waiting for him. She gives him the protection of faith in the form of shoes and stockings. On the other hand, in the material interpretation, the foot and shoe represent a lingam, a joint emblem of penis and vagina.

Later in the same chapter, Stekel talks about the preliminary requisites for a correct interpretation. They are:

1. Knowledge of the dreamer's personality.
2. Of his life.

3. Of his neurotic symptoms.
4. Of the central idea of the dream.
5. Of his mental conflicts.
6. Observing the patient's reactions when he relates his dreams.
7. Observing it when they are interpreted.
8. While doing so, realizing that rejection of the interpretation is an important factor.
9. Imaginative perception of the way the patient's mind functions, avoiding the interference of the psychoanalyst's conflicts. (The psychoanalyst must have been analyzed).
10. The interpretation of a series of dreams makes intuitive interpretation easier.
11. The associations of the patient also express their content through symbols.

Among interesting dreams which Stekel cites in this connection, one includes a first part in which there is a fantasy of being in the father's belly, and a second part of being in the mother's womb.

Some of Stekel's interpretations of dreams are not very convincing or are somewhat unrelated both to the dream and to the associations. They give the impression of being disconnected, ataxic, particularly in comparison to Freud's interpretations on the same subject. In addition, Stekel's constant repetition of the advantages of his method of interpretation as against that of Freud's pupils becomes monotonous.

Stekel's pupils have made valuable contributions to the interpretation of dreams. Most prominent are those of E. A. Gutheil and S. Lowy. A dream related by Gutheil will permit a better understanding of the Stekelian technique of simplification.

158] *I dreamed that I was back at high school and lived in the same boarding house. I saw my schoolmate Douglas with a pipe in his mouth. This surprised me for he had never smoked before.*

Then I was in Elizabeth's house and all her boy friends were there, too. I felt irritated and jealous. I wanted to have her to myself.

Then I dreamed I was with my mother and the assistant principal of my high school. He asked me some questions about Canada and I answered in the negative.

The interpretation given by the author was the following:

1. The dreamer sees himself in the past in his high school days. Simplification: back to the past.
2. He is surprised at seeing his former schoolmate smoking, inasmuch as he had never done so before. Simplification: people are changed.
3. He is alone in his friend Elizabeth's house and is jealous because of her interest in other boys. He complains, "I want to have her to myself." Simplification: rivalry, jealousy, and desire for possession.
4. He sees his mother with the assistant principal (father image). To the latter's question about Canada, the dreamer answers in the negative. (The dreamer's stepfather lives with the patient's mother in Canada.) Simplification: opposition to parents.

To summarize, the patient's thoughts are centered on his childhood. He notices a change of circumstance in his house (people are changed). The patient has the feeling that he has lost his love object, and therefore he develops an opposition toward his parents. The lost love object is the patient's mother, who by chance is also called Elizabeth, and indeed the dreamer's thoughts jump from his friend Elizabeth, and his jealousy of her, toward his mother Elizabeth and Canada.

In this dream one is able to study the patient's main relationship with his parents. One sees the boy's disappointment in his mother (people are changed) and his profound denial of his stepfather (the direction of his thoughts: disappointment and opposition). The simplification of this dream offers considerable insight into the patient's complaints without any assistance from the patient.

Some interpretations of dreams made by Stekel and his

pupils do not differ at all from psychoanalytic interpretations, but in many other dreams, especially if they are complicated, their method fails. Hence, they reach a point during psychoanalysis when, rather than penetrate into the patient's unconscious through associations, they must give up. Then they seek a superficial explanation of the dream, which, although it seems logical and rational, does not uncover the patient's conflicts or the genesis of his neurosis.

Carl Jung is the creator of the school of psychotherapy that he has named "psychosynthesis." He uses a special terminology to designate the various psychic layers: the most superficial are the *mask* or the *persona*, which is the conscious and exterior aspect of the individual, and the *shadow*, the negative element which the individual rejects. Behind these layers are forces with characteristics of the opposite sex, called *anima* in man and *animus* in woman, to correlate them with their opposite sexual aspects. Finally, beyond this individual unconscious is the collective unconscious which is the seat of the *archetypes*.

Dreams must always be examined from two points of view: causality (Freud) and finality. To this end one should inquire what purpose the dream serves and what its aim is, a concept opposed to Freud's idea which is etiological. Thus, interpreting a young man's dream of eating an apple, the genital symbolism of which is known, includes calling his attention to the fact that he has moral forces within himself which he must not forget. Keeping the dream in mind serves, therefore, as a psychic regulator.

There are dreams of various types. Some are compensatory. They introduce into consciousness, thanks to a symbolic arrangement, unconscious material related to the conscious situation. Thus Nebuchadnezzar's dream in the prophecies of Daniel was an effort to compensate for his delusions of grandeur which led to madness. Other dreams are "future-directed" in that they symbolically anticipate a conscious activity in the future. People who live beyond their means have "destructive" dreams which disintegrate, depreciate, and even annihilate.

There are also "reactive" dreams—for example, in traumatic neuroses—and also "prophetic" dreams.

A dreamer awakes from a dream when it has reached its culminating point. As the dream has exhausted its theme, it ends. Awakening is probably due to the sudden cessation of the fascination exercised by the dream; energy thus freed causes the return to consciousness. Jung adds that it is a well-known fact that one awakens frightened at the end of certain dreams.

According to Jung, the defect of psychoanalysis is that it seeks the cause of the symbols of dreams in the particular history of the individual, for it connects all these symbols with the dreamer's experiences or tendencies. Jung claims instead the existence of a collective unconscious in which archetypes would be found, independent of individual experiences. These experiences of the collective unconscious acquire their value when they are treated not analytically but synthetically. Just as psychoanalysis divides symbols into their components, Jung asserts that the synthetic method integrates them into an intelligible and general expression.

Jung agrees with Freud in admitting the existence of wishes in dreams but denies that they are solely wish fulfillments. Nor does he believe that the manifest content of dreams is only the façade of a building which hides everything that lies behind it. He considers it rather as the building itself, even though it is as unintelligible as an ancient text.

Symbols, even those that are relatively constant, do not always have a constant meaning or a sexual one; for instance, the phallic symbols which are said to stand only for the male organ. Nevertheless, from the point of view of the psyche, the penis seems to be in turn the symbol of another difficult-to-define content, as demonstrated by the fact that primitive man makes ample use of phallic symbols without ever confusing the phallus, a ritual symbol, and the penis. Throughout antiquity, the phallus meant the creating *mana*—"that which is unusually potent," according to Lehman's expression—the medicinal and fecundating force also expressed by the bull, the buck, lightning, horseshoes, dancing, magic copulation in the fields, menstruation, and by many other analogies, as also happens in dreams. At the origin of all these analogies, and consequently also of sexuality, there exists an archetypal image with a character difficult to define, and to which the primitive symbol of *mana* seems to be closest psychologically.

Basically, the original psychic fact is of an unsuspected complexity which can only be felt by an intuitive representation of great magnitude. It is precisely for this reason that symbols are required. A dream interpretation by Jung will illustrate this concept.

In the dream a mother is hanged and a horse also kills itself. The mother and the horse are archetypes, and archetypes for Jung are expressions of an innate and basic idea existing in the unconscious. The mother symbol is archetypal and refers to origin, nature, and passive creation, and therefore also to the nature of matter, to the belly (womb), and to the instincts and impulses. The mother in this dream means: unconscious life destroys itself.

A horse is an archetype that is widely found in mythology and folklore. As an animal it represents the non-human psyche, the sub-human, animal side, and therefore the unconscious. This is why the horse in folklore sometimes sees visions, hears voices, and speaks. As a beast of burden it is closely related to the mother-archetype: the Valkyries bear the dead hero to Valhalla, and the Trojan horse encloses the Greeks. Also it has to do with sorcery and magical spells, especially the black, night horse which heralds death.

It is evident, then, that the horse is the equivalent of mother with a slight shift of meaning. The mother stands for life at its origin, and the horse for the merely animal life of the body. If we apply this meaning to the dream, it says: animal life destroys itself.

Jung insists, moreover, that the psychoanalytic interpretation of dreams is unilateral because it is an interpretation on the objective plane: "In order to be complete, there must also be an interpretation on the subjective plane." According to the former interpretation, the psychoanalyst considers dream symbols as representative of real objects; on the subjective plane, the symbols are considered as part of the subject himself. Jung calls this last kind of interpretation a synthetic interpretation, because it separates complexes from their actual causes and reintegrates them in the subject.

A dream of one of Jung's patients demonstrates the difference between his interpretation and a psychoanalytic one. The patient dreamed:

159] *She looked upon Jung as a father and greatly admired him.*

A psychoanalyst would have interpreted this as a transference dream. Jung also did, but added that in this transference the relationship was as follows: daughter—father—God the father. According to Jung, a dream must be considered as a symbol of the patient's ethics, which in this case tended toward God. According to the psychoanalytic interpretation, "on an objective plane," Jung, in the dream, would be a libidinal object; according to the psychosynthetic interpretation, "on a subjective plane," Jung is part of the subject, that is, the patient's ethics. The love of God is a manifestation of the collective unconscious.

In other words, the objective interpretation refers to external objects, while the subjective one refers to the dreamer's own situation. Thus the dream in which a child is run over may mean objectively the dreamer's fear for his child, or subjectively, fear for his own health, the child then being a symbol of a state of mind. Similarly, from a subjective point of view: "Dreams about blacksmiths are dreams of evolution. Our being is surrounded by a fire of suffering, and destiny, an inner force which knows what is best for us, hammers hard. In this way our inner personality is forged."

Jung and his disciples make use of Freud's discoveries without duly acknowledging them, but also without applying Stekel's criticisms. Most of the symbols are interpreted with the same instinctual meaning as psychoanalysis assigns to them, with the addition of a second interpretation unrelated to the instinctual. On the other hand, this instinctual interpretation itself is diluted to erase its precise outlines and bring it close to ambiguous generalities such as a tendency toward evolution or creative forces. Thus the flag is a symbol for intercourse, symbolized by the union of the mast with the cloth; but it could also represent life with its creative bipolarity. In the same way, the myth of the hero killing the dragon to win the virgin represents not only a liberation from a passive mother fixation in order to attain genitality, but also man's passage through the unconscious in order to reach real manhood.

Other interpretations of this kind are those given to numbers. Thus 1 must mean the beginning, egotism, and primitive substance; 2, contradiction, melancholy, and doubt; 3 is the idea, the sacred number, reproducing itself and being born again, also superior intelligence and grace; 4, matter, totality, natural reproduction; 5 is the pentagram, the microcosm, man, the body and the spirit complementing each other; 6, the balance of forces; 7, superior magic power, divine spirit; 8, right and justice, death; 9, total harmony and the whole structure of the psyche.

Jung's psychology, because of its mystical content, has been used in religious writings in an attempt to unite instinctual impulses and dogmatic creeds. Thus John Layard explains the examination of a woman who came to consult him because she was terribly worried, and quite rightly so, about her daughter's mental state. The daughter could not be treated, but the mother had twelve sessions of treatment, almost exclusively devoted to the interpretation of her dreams. Her principal dream had as its central theme the dreamer's sacrifice of a hare that accepted its fate quite willingly. Layard attempts a mystic sort of interpretation. But he does not fail to recognize the instinctual aspect; he merely correlates it with her desire for moral perfection and her aspiration to an ideal life. He concludes that in our present civilized mode of life, the imposition of dogmas has greatly inhibited religious development toward redemption, which exists in the collective unconscious of each human being. He points out that to help the religious perfection of humanity, it is necessary to seek its instinctual source, which must be done with the study of dreams as a basis. He also insists that God spoke to the Prophets in dreams and visions which are now discredited by the Church; Christianity has grown old and it must now be reborn in our dreams, as it appeared previously in the Revelation of St. John, in whose dream processes the presence of the highest spiritual powers may be seen.

An example of Layard's interpretations is the dream in which a mother becomes annoyed with her son because he never obeys her. The mother symbolizes part of the son's psyche which he ignores; hence it becomes something negative for him, instead of helping him in his evolution. Another dream which refers to the marriage of two children would represent "not a sexual union, but a spiritual one, just as the birth of Christ from a pure virgin represents the spiritual rebirth of humanity."

These, then, are interpretations that can only be accepted by those who profess the same ideas as the author. They impress a psychoanalyst as being forced, as intending to impose on the dreamer a series of ideas and standards of behavior that are not found in the latent content of his dreams, although they may well be the consequence of the instinctual elaborations hidden behind this content.

Even so, Layard studies his patients' dreams intensively, trying to find the latent material, not only from the individual point of view but also from the collective. He studies the central animal of the dream, the hare, and to better understand its meaning he collects valuable folklore. He finds that in folk lore the hare is an animal that sacrifices itself voluntarily, often by fire, or by being wounded in the back, in order to benefit somebody. The relationship between the hare and the moon also appears. Of course, according to Layard's ideas, such facts are interpreted as symbolizing the sacrifice of instinctual life for the sake of spirituality, the latter being represented by the moon which shines on the darkness of the soul.

He gives other interesting data, such as the connection

between the hare and witches, whiteness, and snow, and etymologically with Easter, the East, dawn, and spermatic fecundation. In addition, the hare is always represented as having its eyes open: hence the medical name of "lagophthalmos" for this condition.

Psychoanalytically, the following interpretation may be made from this folkloric material: the hare represents the son or daughter united with the mother—the moon—in the absence of the father; a union with oral and genital aspects, the child being either active or passive, as when he has children by the mother-moon, through his sacrifice. The hare's trip to the moon must mean taking refuge in the mother's womb. The union with the mother is often of an oral-digestive type; orality can then either be amply satisfied or be deprived and punished. Punishment may even leave anatomical scars, causing the cleft lip of the hare—harelip—which, according to folklore, was due to a blow the animal received from the moon.

Alfred Adler has the indisputable merit of having formed a psychological school accessible to all minds. In his individual psychology all problems can be solved, even with little knowledge of the facts. This is also the case with dreams, where Adler sees, as he sees in all expressions of the psyche, a manifestation of "power tendency." "The dream shows attempts by the subject to dominate his surroundings and to maintain his power." Thus in psychotherapy the individual psychologist occasionally makes use of dreams to show the patient how he tries to impose himself on others. These tendencies are more often revealed in stereotyped dreams coinciding with the directive lines of the patient's life. Dreams about flying or rising would be characteristic of people who covet a higher position in life; but the fact that one has these dreams shows that he is not altogether sure of his ability to attain it. Dreams about falling into an abyss are typical of people who are afraid of losing their prestige. To miss a train in dreams means to want to avoid some difficulty by being late. Anxiety dreams about fights and shots are dreamed by people who are depressed by

painful situations in their lives, and who fear being involved in unfavorable circumstances from which they will not be able to extricate themselves.

In individual psychology, dreams are of little importance. Their function is reduced to rehearsing projects which the dreamer proposes to carry out afterwards. But they are not even that, since dreams are not intelligible. A dream is only a synchronous movement of our thoughts, our character, and our personality. According to Adler, one can compare it to the smoke of a fire which serves only to indicate in which direction the wind is blowing.

Briefly, individual psychology has little to offer to psychoanalysis, at least as far as dreams are concerned. Jung's work is more valuable, although it sidetracks the investigator from a deep interpretation concerning instinctual life. On the other hand, the writings of Stekel and his pupils are interesting. Besides, the psychoanalyst finds it advantageous to read Stekel, as it shows him a somewhat different point of view. It removes him from his usual techniques, thus allowing him to take a critical look at himself from a distance. It is also useful for exploring other types of interpretation, such as the anagogical, and especially the functional, which are undoubtedly applicable to certain dreams.

Chapter 10

REVERSING FREUD'S THEORY

In "Martin Fierro," the most popular of Argentine epic poems, the author, José Hernandez, describes the state of mind of Martin Fierro's son while he is in prison:

> I can't tell half what I suffered then
> In that cell with its iron grill;
> My sight got so used to locks and bars
> It seemed on my eyes they had left their scars
> And when I shut them, in my sleep
> I kept on seeing them still. . . .

He dreams of "locks and bars," in other words, of prison. His imprisonment is a *traumatic situation.* This is the term Freud used to describe situations that create psychic tensions too intense for the ego either to control or work through. The above dream contains thoughts of a hallucinatory nature about the situation, because, as in all dreams, Martin Fierro's son sees the events of his dream actually happening in exterior reality.

If a *general theory of dreams* were to be based on this particular dream, it would have to postulate that *dreams are psychic phenomena which occur during sleep and reproduce traumatic situations in the form of hallucinatory thoughts.*

Freud describes a similar dream in his *Introductory Lec-*

tures on Psychoanalysis, shown in an engraving by von Schwind, entitled "A Prisoner's Dream." This prisoner is also in a cell, but he dreams far more pleasantly than Martin Fierro's son: while he relaxes, gnomes and fairies are sawing through the bars so that he can escape. We find in this dream the same type of hallucinatory reproduction of the traumatic prison situation, but in addition there are elements of wish fulfillment in the fantasy of being set free. The prisoner represses these thoughts in his waking state because he knows they are impossible, and because his adult mind no longer believes in fairies.

In all his oneiric studies, beginning with the psychoanalysis of his own dreams and the familiar type of "hunger dreams," Freud always insisted on the significance of dreams as hallucinatory gratifications of repressed wishes. It was not until very much later (1920) that he described the operation of traumatic situations in dreams, but he considered these to be extraneous and secondary components of the dream essence—something introduced, as it were, parasitically, an infiltration from contiguous processes.

Freud gave detailed descriptions of the traumatic situations that occur in dreams, but he continued to maintain that they were exceptions. Nevertheless he subsequently modified his theory of dreams as wish fulfillments to one of dreams as *attempted* wish fulfillments.

Drawing upon all Freud's works, and in particular upon his discoveries concerning traumatic situations in dreams and in the origin of neurosis, and drawing also upon my own psychoanalytic experience with dreams, I have put forward the theory, in previous chapters, that traumatic situations are *the basic factor* in the genesis of the dream, and that wish fulfillment plays only a secondary role. It is my further opinion, which I shall once again substantiate, that traumatic situations are responsible for the hallucinations characteristic of dreams. Affect-laden thoughts which occur during sleep create psychical tension which the weakened ego of the sleeper is unable successfully to control or work through. Their impact on the sleeping, weakened ego is as strong, i.e., traumatic, as that of external stimuli on the ego in its waking state, so that the sleeping ego perceives them not just as fantasies but as external environmental realities, thereby committing the error in reality testing known as hallucination.

If this theory is correct, then the question occurs why Freud did not formulate it himself, for it was he who discovered its elements—namely, that the source of dream contents are wish fulfillment and traumatic situations. Possibly there were two reasons. In the first place, Freud came to understand the meaning of dreams through analyzing his own, and like everyone else he must have found it easier to accept them as the fulfillment of wishes, albeit unpleasant ones, rather than the results of traumatic situations of a more painful and overwhelming nature. In the second place, his discovery that dreams are wish fulfillments was such an epic discovery, of such vast importance to the whole of psychoanalysis, that he may have become fixated to it. His enormous and justified satisfaction with his discovery led him to fantasy that one day his house would bear a plaque with the inscription: "In this house, on July 24th, 1895, the secret of dreams was revealed to Dr. Sigm. Freud." And in the foreword to the third English edition of his *Interpretation of Dreams,* he wrote that it was the most valuable of all his discoveries and that "insight such as this falls to one's lot but once in a lifetime."

By means of several examples I shall again demonstrate as simply as possible the fundamental role of traumatic situations in the genesis of dreams. I shall also show how the ego masks these situations in different ways in its efforts to continue sleeping undisturbed.

My first examples are taken from poems, for the simple reason that, unlike real dreams, the dreams in poems are generally described in a way that makes them readily understandable to the reader; consequently they are a good medium for a psychological study of the genesis and meaning of dreams.

In the dream from "Martin Fierro" quoted at the beginning

of this chapter, the actual traumatic situation of being in prison is reproduced in the dream, condensed into the details of the prison locks and bars. The following medieval poem, by Garci Sanchez de Badajoz, dramatizes another type of traumatic situation—the sufferings of a lover in the absence of his beloved:

> Sadness is my companion
> When you are not with me,
> By night and by day
> It is always beside me.
> I live not by day,
> Nor sleep I by night.
> *Should I sleep, I dream of death*
> *I lie dead in the wastelands.*

The absence of the person he loves, "his life," makes the poet feel lifeless. And without his beloved the world is a wasteland. These traumatic reactions of the poet to the absence of his beloved are the cause of his dreams and explain why he dreams of lying dead in a wasteland.

Another poet, Cristobal de Castillejo (c. 1490-1550), experiences a different traumatic situation in real life. He describes it as finding himself:

> On a fierce mountain,
> So hard to climb,
> Without hope of escape
> Till the end of time.

He falls asleep and dreams not of the fierce mountain but of a "pleasant strand." He changes the unhappy traumatic situation into a pleasant one, and we shall see in the following extract from the poem how he does this in a dream:

> . . . And I lay me down in a lovely spot
> In the shade of a hawthorn tree
> Where so pleasant my lot

And so happy was I,
That the thorns changed to roses
As I looked at the sky. . . .

The thorns condense into this one detail all that is painful and unpleasant in his traumatic environmental situation. The ego, in trying to screen the painful traumatic situation, changes the thorns to roses. But it is perfectly clear that the original traumatic situation, and not the changed situation, gave rise to the dream.

When someone has striven to forget a traumatic situation that insists on invading his thoughts, peaceful sleep is impossible. Dreams consist of these painful, traumatic thoughts, which are hallucinated during sleep owing to the special nature of the sleeping psyche. In order to remain asleep and avoid nightmares, the sleeper deceives himself by changing unhappy contents into pleasing oneiric thoughts which can be made conscious and yet allow the dreamer to remain peacefully asleep.

We can presume that there existed in this case a primary original dream which was genetically more important but remained unconscious, and that this primary dream contained the traumatic situation either as it was or condensed into a few details, as in the dream from "Martin Fierro." Another dream later derives from this original primary dream, in which the unpleasant details are masked by more pleasant ones which do not disturb sleep and can therefore easily be made conscious. This is the manifest dream as related by the dreamer. The process is the same as in the genesis of neurotic symptoms.

These derived dreams, which mask the unconscious traumatic ones, lead to the search for pleasure in deceptive dreams, especially in people who cannot alter a real traumatic situation. This is well expressed by the poet Juan Boscan de Almogaver (c. 1495-1542):

Asleep at last
I was content.
And mete it is indeed

That I, ill-starred in life,
Find luck in *lying* dreams.

Let us now pass from the dreams of poets to those of neurotic patients. Here too psychoanalysis shows the primordial importance of the traumatic psychical situation in the genesis of the dream and its subsequent masking by more pleasant things, which give rise to the conscious or manifest content of the dream.

A man who was deeply in debt, and worried about how to pay my fees, had the following dream a few days before he was due to renew a promissory note to a moneylender at an exorbitant rate of interest:

160] *Laura was writing poetry.*

On the surface this was pleasant enough. When I pressed him to associate with the conscious content of the dream, he referred to the moneylender and the promissory note. The moneylender was called Laura. With the poetry he associated his mother's beautiful voice—"sheer poetry" he called it—the voice she had used when he was a child to induce him to comply with an antilibidinal and submissive behavior pattern, which was later to contribute to his failure in life and his falling into the hands of moneylenders. The pleasant conscious aspect of his dream was quite obviously a screen for the trauma of his forthcoming financial subjection to the moneylender and to his analyst, and his previous subjection to his mother. But by masking this unpleasant content he was able to remain asleep and dream.

Another man, who both desired and dreaded psychoanalytic treatment, was in his car one night making love to his girl friend, when suddenly a policeman shone his flashlight on them. The man screamed out with fright and almost had an epileptic fit, but he was finally able with much stammering and stuttering to persuade the policeman not to take them to the police station. Later that night he had the following dream:

161] *I am at a table with other people. Someone lets off a rocket behind me. The others are scared, but I continue to talk calmly.*

Quite obviously his manifest dream masks the actual traumatic event. On hearing the dream one gets the immediate feeling that he recalled and revived his fright while asleep, and this made him dream. He masks this pleasantly by changing the policeman's flashlight and censure into the light and explosion of the rocket; the censured genital situation with his girl friend is transformed in his dream into the more innocent, but nevertheless symbolically related, instinctual situation of eating a meal with other people. His calm reaction in the dream is a clear contradiction of his panicky reaction to the real happening.

A girl who was studying medicine dreamed of what she referred to as "unpleasant things" the night after she first used a contraceptive diaphragm. But there was nothing unpleasant in her dream as she first reported it:

162] *I was buying myself a white pearl necklace. The pearls were enormous.*

From her associations it was clear that these enormous white pearls which she put round her neck were a pleasant screen for the traumatic action of placing over the neck of the uterus what seemed to her an enormous diaphragm full of white jelly. Her introductory comment that she had dreamed of something unpleasant resulted from her dimly apprehended awareness of the traumatic origin of the conscious dream, and from the existence in her unconscious of a primary dream containing the unpleasant content of the originating traumatic situation. A few days later she acted out the traumatic situation in its masked form by buying herself a pair of large white pearl earrings—without realizing the unconscious determining factor.

Another episode in the life of this same patient shows the

interesting way in which she transformed latent traumatic situations into conscious dream contents. One rainy afternoon she had intercourse with her boy friend and on this occasion found it highly unpleasant. This was partly because of her neurosis and partly in response to parental disapproval of her conduct. She thought her boy friend's penis looked like that of an old man, and she was frigid during intercourse. She felt as if her vagina, full of contraceptive jelly, was enormous, and that there was no contact between his penis and the walls of the vagina. The effect of this episode was traumatic. She could not stop thinking of it later when she was trying to sleep, and this produced hypnagogic hallucinations and dreams. One of the hallucinations, as she was dropping off to sleep, was that she "had gone to an optician to buy some eyeglasses." The glasses over her eyes symbolized the diaphragm over the neck of her womb. The traumatic origin of this hallucination can be traced to her having contemplated with distaste both the diaphragm (round in shape like spectacle lenses) and her boy friend's penis. In the hallucination her distasteful contemplation remains unconscious and is substituted for by a symbolism in which both the diaphragm and the act of looking are condensed into the act of putting on eyeglasses at the optician's. (Silberer has used the term "functional phenomenon" for this process to indicate the symbolization of the function itself and not of its content.) The patient, through this hypnagogic image, expressed in a concrete symbolic way that some hours previously she had inserted a diaphragm into her vagina and taken "a dim view" of her boy friend's penis. The optician's shop, which provided the opportunity for her to take this view, was her psychoanalytic treatment.

On the same night she had another hallucination: "people kept coming and offering me boots and more boots." Her association to this was that on "very rainy days, when your boots get very wet, they stretch and feel too big for your feet, which feel uncomfortable as they hardly touch the sides of the boots." She later realized that this symbolized her not having enjoyed intercourse because her vagina was too dilated and too full of contraceptive jelly for her to feel any genital contact of her lover's penis.

When she fell asleep she dreamed:

163] *I was with some Greeks and something happened to do with a laurel wreath.*

She said that this dream seemed to alternate with another about:

164] *Some Romans and a crown of thorns.*

From the interpretation it developed that the round wreaths represented her vagina and the diaphragm, while the thorns represented the spasms of pain caused by the vaginismus during intercourse. Other associations were that the Romans had crowned Jesus with thorns and that this represented her parents' censure, which had been partly responsible for her failure to enjoy intercourse. On the other hand, she felt that the Greeks with their laurel wreaths were permissive of genitality, and that this symbolized her vagina accepting the diaphragm.

It would seem evident that the manifest dream of the Greeks masked the genetic traumatic situation of vaginal pain during intercourse by changing it into something more pleasant. This is why the Greek dream achieved consciousness; the Roman dream, though also of an impersonal nature, was less pleasant because the traumatic genetic situation was more patent, and therefore it tended to remain in the background.

According to Freud, "In dreams the unconscious matter of the id imposes itself on the ego, becomes preconscious and under the rejection of the ego, undergoes those transformations that we know as oneiric deformation. There is no characteristic of dreams that cannot be explained in this manner."

But Freud himself contradicts this by pointing out the existence of hallucination, which is one of the most outstanding characteristics of dreams. Hallucination occurs when the dreamer feels that his dream is actually happening in real life, and it does not consist merely of thoughts, i.e., psychic representations. In other words, the sleeper while dreaming commits serious errors of reality testing, errors which cannot be fully explained in terms of oneiric deformation.

What causes the error that leads to hallucination? According to Freud, the important ego function of distinguishing between fantasy and reality, known as reality testing, is based on the capacity of the ego to reject external stimuli by means of some muscular action. For example, moving a hand to avoid a pinprick. By such means the ego is able to reduce the duration of the stimulus. Internal stimuli, such as hunger, cannot be reduced by this means and consequently are of longer duration.

I first proposed a theory of the origin of reality testing in 1940. Though based on this concept of Freud's, my theory differed from it. My new idea was based on facts such as the attacks of traumatic neurosis in which the traumatized individual hallucinates the intense original trauma. In this case, the stimuli that produce these attacks have such intensity that the ego is incapable of rejecting them, and this leads to the hallucinatory process. According to Freud's theory, this should lead the ego to perceive them as of internal origin, i.e., as mere thoughts, and therefore not to hallucinate them.

Moreover, I maintain that the ego function of reality testing must originate in earliest infancy, before the ego has developed motor innervations sufficiently strong to reject unpleasant external stimuli such as cold or damp. And again, among the external stimuli that assail the infant as he enters postnatal life, surely the first, the most powerful, and often very prolonged are the stimuli accompanying the birth process, against which the infantile ego is completely defenseless. On the other hand, when assailed by stimuli from instinctual drives, the infantile ego is in some way able to deal with them and banish them from consciousness, because it has at its command the defense mechanisms which Freud discovered and described.

The foregoing considerations lead to the conclusion that external reality, from the time of birth, acts against the infant ego, which is gradually building up its reality testing function, by creating a quantity of stimuli which at first the ego can neither reject nor work through. In other words, these external stimuli create what Freud has called traumatic situations, whereas internal stimuli would not, under normal conditions, have the same effect.

The fact, too, that every individual has a better perception of external reality than of his own psyche, would indicate that the ego defense mechanisms are more capable of dealing with internally derived stimuli than with externally derived ones.

Taking the above facts and Freud's teachings into consideration, it would seem necessary to *reverse* Freud's theory of reality testing and to deduce that *the ego considers the stimuli that it is least able to control as coming from external reality, and this gives them a certain traumatic quality for the ego.*

To return to dreams: how to explain their hallucinatory nature, caused by the ego's error of reality testing, which leads it to consider mere thoughts to be real happenings? Within the framework of my reversal of Freud's theory of reality testing, the problem is elucidated. The stimuli that caused the dream are repressed; the ego has found a way of counter-cathecting them during the waking state. But during sleep the ego is partially disintegrated, its defense mechanisms are correspondingly weakened, and it is therefore less able to deal with previously repressed stimuli. During sleep it can neither avoid them nor work through them in the usual way, and therefore a traumatic situation is generated. In other words, according to my theory, the unconscious dream contents now act on the ego in the same intense way as environmental stimuli; the ego, its mental capacities weakened in sleep, mistakenly assigns to them an external origin. Thus the ego hallucinates the dream contents. The hallucinatory nature of dreams derives therefore from the traumatic effects of their contents on the ego.

Nowhere did Freud describe the traumatic origin of dream hallucinations or of hallucinations in general, although he frequently described the traumatic contents of some dreams. And he also taught us that infantile traumata are reproduced in all dreams, not only in traumatic neuroses, and that there are dreams which "in the interest of the psychical binding of traumatic impressions, follow the repetition-compulsion."

According to Freud, such dreams occur when the function of the dream fails. They do not fit into his wish-fulfillment theory. According to him, they occur when the psychic function of sleep is hampered in its work by the infringement upon it of other psychic forces. Because they occur frequently, Freud modified his theory that dreams are wish fulfillments to the theory that they are *attempts* at wish fulfillment. But he attached so little importance to the traumatic contents of dreams that he did not even mention them in the section on dreams in his final work, *An Outline of Psychoanalysis.*

If we accept the theory that all dreams derive from traumatic situations, then the types of dreams referred to above no longer constitute an exception. It is simply easier to trace their traumatic derivations because the original traumatic contents were more intense. One would have to recognize, according to my theory, that there has been a primary hallucination of the latent dream contents. This would occur at the moment when these contents, repressed during the waking state, impinge on the weakened ego which is no longer able to countercathect them during sleep, thereby creating a traumatic situation and with it hallucination. These contents were previously repressed, so the ego must find them unpleasant. Weakened during sleep and no longer able to repress them, the ego must find different and easier defense mechanisms. Thus the unconscious contents of the primitive hallucination are masked by such deformations as condensation, symbolization, and other displacements, including fantasy wish fulfillment. The fulfilled wishes are generally substitutes of previously repressed ones. This masking causes the original contents to become less unpleasant and at times even very pleasant. They can now be admitted to consciousness as the manifest dream content.

The theory of the traumatic origin of dreams would appear to be controverted by dreams which are clearly wish fulfillments, such as "hunger dreams" or "dreams of convenience" in which the dreamer hallucinates that he is performing his daily duties when he is actually still asleep.

There is one type of dream of convenience, however, in which it is relatively easy to show that the generating factor is not wish fulfillment but the impact on the psyche of a traumatic situation. This is the dream of the enuretic who thinks he is in the bathroom, when he is really in bed. Enuresis occurs in individuals who have accepted a submissive or masochistic role in relation to parents or persons in authority.

In the genesis of this type of dream, the important factor is the individual's unconscious acceptance of masochistic behavior patterns which damage the ego by creating unpleasant situations—in this case, urinating in bed. These dreams can be considered wish fulfilling only in the sense that they fulfill hidden masochistic wishes, which because of their traumatic nature can produce hallucinations; they cannot be considered primarily the fulfillment of life wishes. It could even be said that the convenience wishes of the conscious dream are the accomplices of the unconscious masochistic wishes. From the presence of the former we become aware of the latter, which are undoubtedly the most important genetically and responsible for the traumatic situation.

There is a similar mechanism in the hunger dream. When there is no symbolic significance in the manifest content (eating as a symbol for intercourse, for example), such dreams occur in adults or children who have renounced their desires as unattainable or who seek some kind of self-destruction because they feel incapable of satisfying their libidinal drives. This psychically damaging situation acts traumatically on the part of the ego that still aspires to deeper gratification.

As with dreams of convenience, dreams which appear to fulfill the desire to eat are deceptive in that the ego makes use of them to gratify masochistic desires. Take the case of a child who in the hours following an operation was not allowed to drink water to quench his thirst. When he was offered water the next day he refused it, saying that he had drunk jugs of water during the night in his dreams. In the guise of wish fulfillment, this dream signifies the acceptance of very deep instinctual deprivation. In other words, the dream was the very opposite of a libidinal wish fulfillment.

Another instance of the same process can be found in Longfellow's poem "The Slave's Dream":

> Again, in the midst and shadow of sleep,
> He saw his Native Land;
> Wide through the landscape of his dreams
> The lordly Niger flowed;
> Beneath the palm trees on the plain
> *Once more a King he strode;*
> He did not feel the driver's whip,
> Nor the burning heat of day;
> For Death had illuminated the Land of Sleep,
> And his lifeless body lay
> A worn out fetter, that the soul
> Had broken and thrown away!

The conscious content of the slave's dream is that he is dwelling as a king in a delightful place, but in reality he is dying under the lash of the whip and the scorching sun. This dream, on the surface a gratification of pleasurable wishes, is the most effective accomplice of the death wishes against the ego's wish to go on living.

To sum up: the theory that dreams have their origin in traumatic situations is based on a reversal of Freud's theory of reality testing and provides an explanation both for the hallucinatory character of all dreams and for the manifest content of dreams, even of those which do not fit into the wish-fulfillment theory. It can be briefly formulated as follows: *Dreams are hallucinations of unconscious contents which are psychically traumatic to the weakened ego of the sleeper, and which undergo a process of masking before reaching consciousness.* Or to put it even more briefly: *Dreams are hallucinations of masked traumatic situations.*

Bibliography

Ernst Aeppli, *Der Traum und seine Deutung,* Zurich: Eugen Renysch Verlag, 1943

René Allendy, *Rèves expliqués,* Paris: Gallimard, 1938.

Charles Baudoin, *Introduction à l'analyse des rèves,* Geneve: Editions du Mont Blanc, 1945.

A. Béguin, *L'âme romantique et le rève,* Paris: José Corti, 1939.

Paul Bjerre, *Die Träumen als Heilungsweg der Seele,* Leipzig: Rascher Verlag, 1936.

Walter Bonime, *The Clinical Use of Dreams,* New York: Basic Books, 1962.

Robert Bossard, *Psychologie des Traumbewussteins,* Zurich: Rascher Verlag, 1951.

M. F. DeMartino, *Dreams and Personality Dynamics,* Springfield, Ill.: Charles C. Thomas, 1959.

Charles Fisher, "Dream Images and Perception: A Study of Unconscious-Preconscious Relationships," *Journal of the American Psychoanalytic Association,* 1956, *4,* 5-48.

———, "A Study of the Preliminary Stages of the Construction of Dreams and Images," *Journal of the American Psychoanalytic Association,* 1957, *5,* 5-60.

———, "Psychoanalytic Implications of Recent Research on Sleeping and Dreaming," *Journal of the American Psychoanalytic Association,* 1965, *13,* 197-303.

Robert Fliess, *The Revival of Interest in the Dream,* New York: International Universities Press, 1953.

Nandor Fodor, *New Approaches to Dream Interpretation,* New York: Citadel, 1951.

Thomas M. French, *The Integration of Behavior;* Vol. II: *The Integrative Process in Dreams,* Chicago: University of Chicago Press, 1952.

——— and Erika Fromm, *Dream Interpretation: A New Approach,* New York: Basic Books, 1964.

Sigmund Freud, standard edition, London: Hogarth Press, 1955-1965:

1900—"The Interpretation of Dreams," Vol. IV

1900—"A Premonitory Dream Fulfilled," Vol. IV

1901—"On Dreams," Vol. V

1905—"Fragment of an Analysis of a Case of Hysteria," Vol. VII

1911—"Dreams in Folklore," Vol. XII (with D. E. Oppenheimer)

1912—"The Handling of Dream Interpretation in Psychoanalysis," Vol. XII

1913—"The Occurrence in Dreams of Material from Fairy Tales," Vol. XII

1913—"An Evidential Dream," Vol. XII

1917—"A Metapsychological Supplement to the Theory of Dreams," Vol. XIV

1916-1917—"Dreams" (Chapter 2 in "A General Introduction to Psychoanalysis"), Vol. XVI

1918—"An Infantile Neurosis," Vol. XVII

1920—"Beyond the Pleasure Principle," Vol. XVIII

1922—"Dreams and Telepathy," Vol. XVIII

1923—"Remarks on the Theory and Practice of Dream Interpretation," Vol. XIX

1923—"Joseph Popper-Lynkeus and the Theory of Dreams," Vol. XIX

1925—"Some Additional Notes on Dream Interpretation as a Whole," Vol. XIX

1929—"A Letter to Maxime Leroy," Vol. XXI

1933—"New Introductory Lectures on Psychoanalysis; Revision of the Theory of Dreams; Dreams and Occultism," Vol. XXII

1940—"An Outline of Psychoanalysis—Chapter 5: Dream Interpretation as an Illustration," Vol. XXIII

Emil Gutheil, *The Language of the Dream*, New York: Macmillan, 1939.

————, *The Handbook of Dream Analysis*, New York: Liveright, 1951.

J. A. Hadfield, *Dreams and Nightmares*, London: Penguin Books, 1954.

Calvin S. Hall, *The Meaning of Dreams*, New York: Harper, 1953.

E. Harms, ed., *Problems of Sleep and Dreams in Children* (Vol. II of *Monographs on Child Psychiatry*), New York: Pergamon Press, 1964.

Ignaz Jezower, *Das Buch der Traume*, Berlin: Ernst Rowohlt, 1927.

Ernest Jones, *On the Nightmare*, London: Hogarth Press, 1931.

Richard M. Jones, *Ego Synthesis in Dreams,* Cambridge, Mass.: Schenkman, 1962.

C. G. Jung, *L'homme à la découverte de son âme,* Geneve: Editions du Mont Blanc, 1946.

————, *Psychology of the Unconscious,* London: Routledge and Kegan Paul, 1946.

F. Kehrer, *Wach- und Wahrträumen bei Gesunden und Kranken,* Leipzig: Thieme, 1935.

Werner Kemper, *Der Traum und seine Bedeutung,* Hamburg: Rowohlt, 1955.

Olga Freiin Von Keonig-Fachsenfeld, *Wandlungen des Traumproblems von der Romantik bis zur Gegenwart,* Stuttgart: Ferdinand Enke, 1935.

C. W. Kimmins, *Children's Dreams,* London: Allen and Unwin, 1937.

Nathaniel Kleitman, *Sleep and Wakefulness,* Chicago: University of Chicago Press, 1963 (2nd ed.).

Bertram D. Lewin, *Dreams and the Uses of Regression,* New York: International Universities Press, 1958.

S. Lowy, *Foundations of Dream Interpretation,* London: Routledge and Kegan Paul, 1942.

R. L. Mégroz, *The Dream World,* New York: Dutton, 1939.

Pedro Mescguer, *El secreto de los sueños,* Madrid: Editorial Razon y Fe, 1956.

A. Leo Oppenheim, *The Interpretation of Dreams in the Ancient Far East,* Philadelphia: American Philosophical Society, 1956.

J. R. Otaola, *El análisis de los sueños,* Barcelona: Argos, n.d.

Jean Piaget, *Play Dreams and Imitation in Childhood,* New York: Norton, 1951.

Otto Potzl, "The Relationship Between Experimentally Induced Dream Images and Indirect Vision," *Psychological Issues,* 1960, 2.

A. J. J. Ratcliff, *The Nature of Dreams,* London: Thomas Nelson, 1939.

Geza Roheim, *The Gates of the Dream,* New York: International Universities Press, 1952.

Ella Sharpe, *Dream Analysis,* London: Hogarth Press, 1937.

Wilhelm Stekel, *Die Sprache des Traumes,* Wiesbaden: Bergmann, 1911.

————, *The Interpretation of Dreams,* New York: Liveright, 1943.

W. O. Stevens, *The Mystery of Dreams,* London: Allen and Unwin, 1950.

A. Stocker, *Les rèves et les songes,* St. Maurice: Editions Oeuvre St. Augustin, 1945.

Ania Teillard, *Traumsymbolik,* Zurich: Rascher Verlag, 1944.

———, *Le rève, une porte sur le réel,* Paris: Librairie Stock, 1951.

Mauro Torres, *Dialéctica de los sueños,* Bogotá: Universidad Libre de Colombia, 1962.

Julian Varendonck, *The Psychology of Day-Dreams,* New York: Macmillan, 1921.

Werner Wolff, *The Dream: Mirror of Conscience,* New York: Grune and Stratton, 1952.

Clement Wood, *Your Dreams and What They Mean,* New York: World, 1931.

Ralph L. Woods, *The World of Dreams,* New York: Random House, 1947.

Indexes to Dreams

A. SYMBOLS

(The numbers here refer to dreams and not to pages.)
These symbols usually appear in the manifest content of the dreams, but some appear only in the associations mentioned.

Ants, 97: criticism
Apron, 16: hymen
Armchair, 10: breasts
Arms, 2, 41: penis; arms hanging, 2: impotence
Arrive somewhere, 76: orgasm

Badly dressed, 22: defloration
Balloon, 84: belly
Bandages, 85, 86: inhibitions
Banknotes, 3: semen
Bars, 49: penis
Basin of water, 8: mind
Bathe oneself, 4: to be psychoanalyzed
Bathing suit, 103: coitus
Bathrobe, 40: naked; strange bathrobe, 40: genital excitation
Bed, 9: psychoanalytic couch
Beginning of season, 11: marriage
Bellows, 1: penis
Bench, 52: bed
Bird, 5: thoughts; 10: child; 45: penis; white bird, 5: leucorrhea
Bird's beak, 91: female genitals
Blanket, 80: genital excitation
Block, 98: penis
Blood, 57: semen
Boat, 2: female genitals
Boats, small, 24: children
Boil, 110: genital excitation
Book, 35: penis; 124: anus
Bookcase, 18: mind
Box, 13: female genitals; 127: urine bladder; 3: testicles
Boxes, 2: testicles
Boy, 148: Jesus
Bread, 37, 60: penis
Break, 15: defloration
Bricks, 131: breast
Broken, 12, 16, 21, 71: defloration
Brother, 65: penis

Bud, 156: virginity
Butchers, 11: female genitals
Buttons, 27: children, breasts
Buying, 18, 43: coitus; buying something, 114: getting married

Cactus, 31: penis
Cage, 45: female genitals
Cake, 101: semen
Canal, 102: female genitals
Candy, 72: orgasm
Cap, 4: contraceptive
Car, 57: masturbation; 111, 112: woman
Carrot, 86: male genitals
Cats, 84: children
Ceiling, 5: head; 6: upper part of vagina
Child, 55: penis
Cigarette, 133: penis
Cinema, 74: genital excitation
Circle revolving, 138: intercourse
Clam, 91: female genitals
Close, 13: break off genital relationship
Clothes, 79: genital excitation; 92: penis
Colonial patio, 8: psychoanalyst
Color dreams, 123, 124, 125, 126: anal excremental contents
Communism, 62: marriage
Cone, 12: female genitals
Cord, 43: penis
Corridor, 6, 21: vagina
Cover of book, 35: prepuce
Cross the room, 69: coitus
Curling hair, 73: female orgasm
Curved, 44: erection

Dance, 74: coitus
Daughter (younger), 74, 81, 87, 90, 101: female genitals
Devil, 43: sexually excited man
Dirty, 16: deflorate
Display of lights, 9: penis
Doctor, 133: mother
Doll, 19: hymen
Door, 11, 18, 45, 52: female genitals; door of exit, 108: orgasm
Drain, 11: vagina
Dress, 82: female genitals; 155: hymen; put on, 78: genital excitation; white, with lace, 17: coitus; short, 42: exhibition
Drinking, 154: intercourse
Drop into, 49: ejaculation

Eat, 91, 101: coitus
Embrace daughter, 83: pregnancy
Empress, 152: mother-in-law
Enormous, 53, 98: erection
Enter and leave, 45: coitus
Enter room, 115: coitus
Erection, 122: difficulty in getting up
Evening dress, 53, 66, 111: genital excitation; tails, 66: male genitals
Evening suit, 47: naked, excited
Eyelid, 150: prepuce
Eyes, round, 29: testicles

Fall, 75, 94, 97: coitus
Father, 157: God
Feather, 52: penis
Fire, 61: genitality
Firearms, 24: milk
Fish, 8: thoughts
Five errors, 58: five fingers
Flannel suit, 41: caresses
Flower vase, 12: female genitals
Frame, 18: hymen

Frigidaire, 71: frigidity
Fruit, 18: male genitals

Gate, 46: female genitals
Get up, 33, 46, 65, 69: erection
Get wet, 81: become pregnant
Girl, 140: neurosis
Go in street car, 109: coitus
Go on trip, 73: coitus
Go up in elevator, 82, 111: coitus
Going to church, 36: coitus
Goods, 132: wife
Grapes, on the stem, 91: male genitals
Greet, 33: to become excited

Hair on nape of neck, 87: pubic hair
Hall, 1: female genitals
Hand, 52: female genitals
Handle, 39: prepuce
Hands, 88: breasts
Hat, 52: penis
Head, 81: female genitals
Hindus, 49: instincts
Horse, 46, 119, 151: penis; white horse, 97: sexually excited man
Hospital, 33: psychoanalysis
House, 10, 18: body; 70, 71, 78: woman

Ice cream, 39: frigidity
Island, 14: female genitals

Jug, 71: vagina
Jungle, 102: female genitals

King, 139: patient; 139: neurosis
Knife, 53: penis

Lampshade, 63: female genitals; 63: penis
Lance, 5: penis
Land, 25: mother
Lease, 78: ejaculation
Legs, 64: penis
Lice, 87: genital excitation
Lie down, 2, 4, 5, 9: to be psychoanalyzed
Light, 111, 112: love
Lighthouse, 148: church
Lion, 108: sexually excited man
Lions and tigers, 49: ejaculation
Load, 32: male genitals
Lose a tooth, 129: castration
Luminous sign, 90: male genitals

Madman, 8: psychoanalyst
Maid, 9: psychoanalyst
Marmalade, 60: genital pleasure
Masts, 24: breasts
Material, length of, 48: male genitals
Meeting, 79: coitus
Meteor, 136: pregnancy
Milk, 110: semen
Ministry of Interior, 38: mind
Mirror, 15: hymen
Mosquito, 6: genital excitation
Mother, 29, 83: womb; 123: psychoanalyst; 123: patient; 147: neurosis; 157: Virgin Mary
Mother-in law, 29: superego
Mouth, 27, 101: female genitals

Nape of neck, 87: upper part of vagina
Neck, 35: prepuce
Necklace, 162: contraceptive diaphragm
New, 20: vagina
Niece, 109: female genitals
Nipple, 135: penis

Nose, 29: penis
Nymph, 44: female genitals

Old lady, 105: mother
Old woman, 147: psychoanalyst
Open letter, 156: defloration
Opening and closing umbrella, 100: coitus
Opening drain, 11: defloration

Paint, dirty oneself with, 82: become pregnant
Pajamas, 4: love, menstruation
Palisade, 136: breast; 136: teeth
Paper, 20: hymen
Paradise, 5: genital pleasure
Parents, 97: conscience
Party, 66, 72: coitus
Peach stone, 87: testicles
Pearl, 162: contraceptive diaphragm
Pencil, 125: penis
People, 71: genital excitement
Phonograph record, 23: female genitals
Pistol, 32: penis
Pit, 49: female genitals
Plant, 10: female genitals
Play piece of music, 58: masturbate
Poetry, 160: voice
Posters, 104: penis
Pour water, 40: coitus
Powder, 1: semen
Powder compact, 15: female genitals
Prepare cup of tea, 78: female orgasm
Present from mother, 12: female genitals
President, 69: penis
Prick with fork, 8: psychoanalyze
Purse, 99: female genitals
Pursue, 108: coitus
Pursuing, 98: coitus
Put on wedding dress, 17: live with
Put white powder, 1: coitus

Quite big, 29: erection

Railings, thin black, 1: pubic hair
Rain, 73: ejaculation
Raspberries, 25: breasts
Red, 4, 21, 26, 121: menstruation; 7: tenderness
Ride in car, 23, 50: coitus
Ride on horseback, 119: genital excitation
Ring, 34: prepuce
Room, 5, 69: female genitals; 80: mental attitude
Rope, 63: penis
Roses, 79: orgasm; 135: nipple; red roses, 26: menstruate
Run over, 95: coitus
Running, 96, 98: coitus

Sailing boat, 24: woman
Scotch, 7: genital excitement
Screen, 133, 134, 135, 136: breast
Sentence, 113: marriage
Servant, 5, 6: psychoanalyst; 161, neurosis; 71, 105: female genitals; 6: husband
Shake hands, 59: masturbate
Shirt, 66: penis; starched, 47, 66: erection
Shoes, 20, 123: female genitals; 43: penis; 123: rectum, anus
Shoes falling off; 43: impotence
Shoot, 77: coitus
Sister (younger), 16, 18: female genitals

Sisters, 52: breasts
Sit next to, 109: coitus; in low chair, 8: to psychoanalyze
Sixth, 118: genitality
Slap, 62: masturbate; slap a child, 89: masturbation
Slippers, 107: testicles
Small men, 30: penis
Smell, 26: menstruation
Soap oneself, 11: masturbation
Son, 29: male genitals; 101: penis; 152: husband
Spill wine, 101: ejaculation
Spoons, 39: penis
Staircase, 41, 43: coitus
Stamp, 149: hymen
Stick posters, 104: coitus
Stiff, 47: erection
Storm, 147: neurosis
Straw, 61: masturbation
Surgical operation, 85: coitus
Swimming pool, 11: mother
Sword, 44: penis

Table, 70, 134, 161: bed
Taking care of child, 55: masturbation
Tall, 31: erection
Tears, 28: menstruation
Teeth, 27: children
Tent, 126: womb
Things, 70: genital excitation
Thorns, 31: sorrows
Three, 48, 49, 66, 68, 113, 125: male genitals
Three horses, 144: trigeminal nerve
Throat, 56: penis
Throw oneself, 93, 94: coitus
Tiger, 100: mother
To be cured, 87: coitus
To be in paradise, 5: coitus
To go on board, 2, 47: coitus
To pass an exam, 117: coitus
To spear; 5: coitus
To water, 10: coitus
Tooth, 129: penis
Toothbrush, 67: penis
Top shelf of cabinet, 67: mouth
Torn dress, 155: defloration
Train, to catch the, 120: to die
Travel, 50, 51: coitus
Trunk, 19: female genitals
Turk, 44: sexually excited man
Turnips, 86: male genitals
Two, 32: woman; 24, 27: breasts: two doors, 11: vulva

Umbrella, 100: male genitals
Unable to dance, 74: frigidity
Unbuttoned, 36: circumcision

Vacation, 103: coitus
Violet, 125: rape
Vomit, 55: ejaculate; 125: defecate

Walk, 41, 64: coitus
Watch, 34: male genitals
Water, 40, 81: semen; 127: urine
Wedding dress, 17: coitus
Well, 8: female genitals
White, 87: leucorrhea; 97, marriage; 16, 44: virgin; 133, 134, 136: breast
Winding screw, 34: penis
Window, 30, 73, 125: female genitals
Wine, 101: semen
Wings, 30: erection
Woman, 33: homosexuality; 62: penis

Yellow, 7: coldness

B. THINGS SYMBOLIZED

(The numbers here refer to dreams and not to pages.)
These things usually appear in the manifest content of the dreams, but some appear only in the associations mentioned.

MIND

Ideas: bird, 5; fish, 8
Inhibitions: bandages, 85, 86
Mind: basin with water, 8; Ministry of the Interior, 38
Neuroses: birthplace, 119; girl, 140; king, 139; mother, 123, 147; servant, 141; storm, 148
Psychoanalyst: colonial patio, 8; madman, 8; old woman, 147; servant, 5, 6, 9
Superego: father, 97; mother-in-law, 29
To be psychoanalyzed: hospital, 35; lie down, 2, 4, 5, 9; prick, 8; sit on a low stool, 8; spear, 5; take a bath, 4

BODY

Body: house, 10, 12
Head: ceiling, 6
Teeth: palisade, 136
Urethral and anal: book, 124; box, 127; brown, 123; color, 123, 124, 125, 126; shoes, 123; water, 127; window, 125

GENITALITY

Bed: bench, 52; table, 70, 134, 161
Coitus—actions: buying, 18; dancing, 74; getting cured, 86; going for a vacation, 103; open and close umbrella, 100; putting on wedding dress, 17; stick posters, 104; taking an exam, 117; *cohabitation*—revolving circle, 138; to be in paradise, 5; to come in and go out, 45; to cross a room, 69; to go into a room, 115; *eating*—eat, 91, 101; *falling*—to fall, 75, 94, 97; to throw oneself, 93, 94; *going up or down*—going up in a lift, 82, 111; *party*—party, 66, 72; *run*—to be run over, 95; to run, 96, 98; to pursue, 108; *shoot*—shoot, 77; to pour water, 40; to put white

powder, 1; to spear, 5; to water, 10; *vehicles*—to go on a trip, 73; to go on board, 2, 47; to go to church, 36; to ride in a car, 23, 50; to ride in a tram, 109; to walk, 41, 64; *miscellaneous*—bathing suit, 103; lace dress, 17; staircase, 41, 43; surgical operation, 85; wedding dress, 17

Contraceptive diaphragm: necklace, 162; pearl, 162

Genital excitation—animals: horse, 97, 119; lice, 87; lion, 108; mosquitoes, 6; *clothing*—blanket, 80; clothes, 79; dressing oneself, 78; evening dress, 53; evening gown, 66; strange bathrobe, 40; *heat*—boil, 110; electricity, 49; fire, 61, 129; *people*—devil, 43; people, 71; Turk, 44; *miscellaneous*—to greet, 33

Genitality: sixth, 118; things, 70

Marriage: beginning of the season, 11; buy something, 114; cinema, 74; communism, 62; house, 115; sentence, 113; white, 97

Orgasm and pleasure: arriving somewhere, 76; candy, 72; curl hair, 73; fire, 129; marmalade, 60; prepare cup of tea, 78; roses, 79

MAN

Castration: to lose a tooth, 129

Circumcision: cut, 37; unbuttoned, 36

Ejaculation: to drop into, 49; to go away, 78; to rain, 73; to spill wine, 101; to take a shower, 81; to vomit, 55

Erection: curved, 44; enormous, 53, 98; hard, 47; lions and tigers, 49; quite big, 29; starched shirt, 47, 66; tall, 31; to get up, 46, 65; to rise, 33, 69; wings, 30

Impotence: falling off, 43; hanging arms, 2; hanging head, 2

Male genital organs: bunch of grapes, 91; carrot, 86; fruit, 18, 42; head, 102; illuminated sign, 90; length of material, 48; tails, 66; three, 48, 66, 68, 125; turnips, 86; umbrella, 100; watch, 34

Masturbation—child: look after a child, 55; slap a child, 89; *hand*—five mistakes (fingers), 58; play a piece of music, 58; pull the rope, 63; shake hands, 59; soap oneself, 11; *miscellaneous*—car, 57; slap, 62; straw, 61

Penis—animals: bird, 45; horse, 46, 119, 151; spider, 63; *clothing*—hat, 52; shirt, 66, 92; shoes, 43; *parts of the body*—arm, 41; head, 2; legs, 64; nose, 29; throat, 56; *people*—boy, 55; brother, 65; small men, 30; son, 101; woman, 62; *through similarity of sound in Spanish*—bread, 37, 60; *weapons*—knife, 53; lance, 5; pistol, 32; sword, 44; *miscellaneous*—bars, 49; bellows, 1; block, 98; book, 35; cactus, 31; cigarette, 133; cord, 43; display of lights, 9; feather, 52; lift, 43; load, 32; posters, 104; rope, 63; screw, 34; spoons, 39; three, 49

Prepuce: book cover, 35; eyelid, 150; handle, 34; neck, 35; ring, 34

Semen: banknotes, 3; blood, 57; cake, 101; milk, 110; powder, 1; water, 40, 81; wine, 101
Testicles: boxes, 2, 3; peach stones, 87; round eyes, 39; slippers, 107; spectacles, 106

WOMAN

Breasts: armchairs, 10; bricks, 136; buttons, 27; hands, 88; masts, 24; meteor, 136; palisade, 136; raspberries, 25; screen, 133, 135, 136; sisters, 52; two, 24, 27, 52; white, 133, 134, 136
Defloration: badly dressed, 22; broken, 12, 15, 16, 21, 71; dirty, 16; open drain, 11; open letter, 156; torn dress, 155
Female genital organs—building: corridor, 7, 21; door, 18, 45, 52; hall, 1; room, 5, 69; tent, 126; two doors, 11; window, 30, 73, 126; *clothing*—dress, 82; shoes, 20, 123; *landscape*—canal, 102; gate, 46; island, 14; jungle, 102; *parts of the body*—head, 81; mouth, 27, 101; *people*—daughter (younger), 74, 87, 89, 90, 101; niece, 109; nymphs, 44; servant, 71, 105; sister (younger), 74, 87, 89, 90, 101; *receptacles*—boat, 2; box, 13; cage, 45; crown, 164; drain, 11; flower vase, 12; jug, 71; powder compact, 15; purse, 99; trunk, 19; well, 8; wreath, 163; *miscellaneous*—butcher, 11; cone, 12; phonograph records, 23; plant, 10; present from mother, 12; two, 32
Frigidity: frigidaire, 72; ice cream, 39; unable to dance, 74
Husband: servant, 6; son, 152
Hymen: apron, 16; doll, 19; dress, 155; frame, 18; mirror, 15; paper, 20; stamp, 149
Menstruation: pajamas, 4; red, 21, 26, 121; roses, 26; smell, 26; tears, 28
Milk: firearms, 24; fuel, 24
Mother or maternity: doctor, 133; land, 25; old lady, 105; swimming pool, 11
Nipple: roses, 135
Pregnancy: embrace daughter, 83; get dirty with paint, 82; get wet, 81; meteor, 136; pick up daughter, 83
Pubic hair: hair on nape of neck, 87; thin black railings, 1; wire netting, 11
Rape: violet, 125
Son or child: bird, 10; buttons, 27; cats, 84; psychoanalyst, 28; small boats, 24; teeth, 27
Uterus: balloon, 84; mother, 29, 83
Virginity: bud, 156; new, 20; white, 11, 44
Woman: car, 111, 112; goods, 132; house, 70, 71, 78; sailing boat, 24

Index to the Book

Adler, Alfred, 174, 192-193
Analysis: auto-, 70; didactic, 70
Asenirsky, Eugene, 60

Betlheim, Stjepan, 45

Castration: actual, 181; fear of 81, 94, 125, 126, 131
Childhood, importance in dreams, 57
Circumcision, 81, 82, 83
Coitus, 30, 45, 46, 52, 79, 83, 84, 86, 87, 89, 90, 91, 95, 96, 98, 100, 101, 111, 114, 116, 169. *See also* Intercourse.
Condensation, 43, 205
Counter-cathexis, 144-156, 204

Day residues, 56-57, 62, 71, 77, 89, 90, 113, 114, 116, 117, 168
Debacker, 129
Defloration, 73, 75, 76, 99, 179, 181
Dement, William, 60
Desires, unconscious, 60. *See also* Wishes.
Displacement, 44, 55, 113, 118, 136, 205
Don Quixote, 95-96
Dramatization, of desires, 25
Drawings, of dreams, 28, 32, 56; used in experiments, 62-63
Dream of Poets, The, 175
Dreams: are hallucinations, 21, 208; as *attempted* wish fulfillment, 195; as wish fulfillment, denied, 21, 128; attracted to disagreeable things, 129-134; of compliance, 69; of convenience, 58-59; cowardice of, 130-133, 137-138; distortion of, 43; divided into components, 27; dream screen, 157-170; dream work, 42-62; of enuretics, *see* Enuresis; erotic transference dream, 109; excremental meaning of colored, 122-127; genesis of, 63, 141-156; infantile, 42; number in a night, 61; of opposition, 69; psychoanalytical interpretation of,

21-41; repressed wishes in, 23; reproduce infantile traumatic experiences, 128; satisfy sense of duty and organic need, 58; secondary revision, 32, 52-53; sexual meaning, 24; technique of interpretation, 65-70, 182-186; traumatic situations, due to, 128-140; try to pacify enemies of sleep, 59; two sources: present and childhood, 57; unpleasant in 58 percent of all adults', 129
Dreams and Intuition, 178
Dreams of a Homosexual Man, 182

Ego, 47, 139, 142-155 *passim*, 167, 195, 196, 202, 203, 204, 206, 207; relaxes at night, 22, 36, 152; represses wishes, 21-22; super-ego, 47, 55, 64, 71, 96, 117, 128, 129, 131; "The Ego and the Id," 64
Eissler, Kurt, 79
Enuresis, nocturnal, 59, 133, 139, 206
Erotic gratification, 117

Farber, Leslie H., 45
Fisher, Charles, 45, 61
Fixation, father, 180; genital, 180; mother, 190
Freud, Sigmund, 50, 56, 57, 58, 64, 120, 128, 129, 131-133, 140, 142, 143, 145, 147, 149, 150, 151, 152, 155, 174, 175, 184, 186, 194-195, 196, 202, 203, 204, 205; Freud's theory reversed, 194-208
Frigidity, 94, 98, 99, 115, 118, 165, 176, 182, 201

Genesis of dream hallucination, 141-156; of dreams, 63; basic factor in, 128-140, 195
Genital: act, 108; activity, 123, 125; conflicts, 104-127; contact, 202; excitation, 106, 107; frustrations, 171; genitality, 118, 162, 181, 190, 202; organs, 25, 29, 31, 40, 41, 48, 51, 52, 71-81 *passim*, 85, 87, 89, 91, 94, 95, 98, 100, 105, 106, 108, 111, 112, 113, 114, 119, 126, 165; potency, 161, 167; response, 117; satisfaction, 99, 168; symbol, 45; symbolism in dreams, 71-103; thoughts, 39; wishes, 37
Glauber, I. P., 163-164, 165
Gutheil, E. A., 184

Hallam, Florence, 129
Hallucinations, 22, 23, 139, 202, 203, 204, 205, 207, 208; hallucinatory gratifications, 195
Heilbrunn, Gert, 171
Homosexual, 69, 79, 103, 119, 155, 176, 182
Hug-Hellmuth, Hermine von, 23
Hymen, 73, 75, 179
Hypnosis, 45-46, 54

Id, 64, 152, 155; "The Ego and the Id," 64

Impotence, 94-95, 96, 97, 98, 100, 125, 176, 180
Incestuous, 89
Intercourse, 30, 31, 35, 72, 73, 74, 82-92 *passim*, 98, 100, 101, 106, 113, 114, 116, 126, 169, 171, 182, 201, 202, 206; anal, 122, 123, 124. *See also* Coitus; Sexual relations.
Interpretation of Dreams, 175
Introductory Lectures on Psychoanalysis, 194-195
Isakower, Otto, 157; phenomenon, 170-173

Jones, Ernest, 52
Jung, Carl G., 174, 183, 186-190, 193

Kleitman, Nathaniel, 60
Korsakoff's syndrome, 45
Kubie, Lawrence S., 159-160, 163, 164

Language of Dreams, The, 174
Latent: content, 48, 65, 80, 106, 109, 123, 154, 205; material, 180; meanings, 66, 89, 104, 107; repressed desires, 153; thoughts, 42-44, 55, 56, 58, 60, 107; trauma, 153, 168, 182
Layard, John, 190-192
Lewin, Bertram D., 157-160, 161, 163, 164, 166, 167, 168, 170
Libido, 41, 106; libidinal gratification, 108
Lorca, García, 87
Lowy, Samuel, 184

Manifest content, 42-44, 52, 53, 54, 57, 59, 62, 65, 80, 89, 104, 108, 121, 138, 154, 158, 206, 207
"Martin Fierro," 194, 195, 196-197, 198
Masking, 71, 111, 199, 200, 205
Masochism, 88, 96, 120, 124, 126, 129-130, 176, 206, 207
Masturbation, 72, 79, 91, 92, 93, 94, 106, 131, 171

Narcissism, 168
Necrophilic act, 91
Neurosis, 30, 33, 55, 66, 67, 129, 134, 135, 137, 138, 175, 176, 178, 186, 199, 201; traumatic, 144-146, 187, 203; neurotic inhibition, 130
Nocturnal emission, 59

Ocular movements, 60-62
Odyssey, 85, 86
Oedipus, 89; complex, 131; objects, 124; oedipal father, 86
Oneiric. *See* Hallucinations.
Outline of Psychoanalysis, 205

Paranoic, 155
Perception, inner and outer, 142-156
Phallic symbol, 29, 35, 48, 81, 83, 105, 107, 109, 110, 124, 167, 187
Poetzl, Otto, 56, 62
Psyche, 68, 69, 144, 151, 175, 187, 198, 206
Psychoanalytic: interpretation, deviations from, 174-193;

treatment, use of dreams in, 65-70
Psychosis, 96, 155
Psychosynthesis, 186-190

Rank, Otto, 52
Reich, Wilhelm, 69
Reik, Theodor, 145, 151
Repressions, 66, 67; repressed desires, 153; repressed thoughts, 68
Resistance, psychic, 68
Rycroft, Charles, 167-168

Sachs, Hanns, 52
Sadger, J., 177-178
Sadism, 22, 23, 91, 129-130
Sadomasochistic sexual act, 105
Schizophrenics, 167, 176
Schroetter, Karl, 45
Sexual: activity, 47, 62, 92, 112; desires, 56, 90, 93, 95, 110, 111, 115, 116; excitement, 48, 49, 52, 59, 81, 87, 91, 100, 101, 115, 116, 119, 131; experiences, infantile, 107; fantasies, 100; gratification, 104, 105; inhibitions, 104, 108; instincts, 88; intercourse, *see* Intercourse; organs, 116; relations, 36, 72, 74, 118, 135, 162, 179, 181; satisfaction, 99, 100; surrender, 50, 52, 98; thoughts, 56; union, 191
Silberer, Herbert, 183, 201
Simplification method of Stekel, 175-186
Spira, Marcela, 172
Stammering, 176
Stekel, Wilhelm, 174-186, 189, 193
Subliminal visual stimulation, 62
Symbolic representation, masks wishes, 24-25
Symbolization, 44-52, 55, 205

Transference, 27, 32, 34, 36, 37, 38, 40, 41, 68, 69, 90, 93, 189
Traumata, psychic, 63, 68, 128-140; traumatic situation, 195-202 *passim*, 205, 206, 207, 208; basic in genesis of dreams, 128-140

Virginity, loss of, 73, 74, 75, 181

Weed, Sarah, 129
Wishes: death, 207; disguised in dreams, 23-24; dramatized in dreams, 25; often instinctual, 22; repressed in dreams, 23; sexual, 24; unconscious, 57-58, 60; wish fulfillment, 21, 128, 138, 139, 140, 141, 187, 196, 207-208; *attempted*, 195, 205
Word-association tests, 62-63